**WHEN THE LIGHTS GO OUT,
THE LAUGHTER STARTS!**

FOR ANYONE WHO HAS EVER
WONDERED . . .

WHY SEX IS LIKE A GAME
OF BRIDGE . . .

WHY RONALD MCDONALD
GOT BUSTED . . .

HOW YOU CAN TELL IF YOUR
GIRL IS TOO FAT . . .

AMERICA'S #1 JOKESTER
BARES IT ALL!

SO, CUDDLE UP WITH LARRY WILDE'S
HOTTEST COLLECTION EVER—

**THE ABSOLUTELY LAST OFFICIAL
SEX MANIAC'S JOKE BOOK**

THE Absolutely Last OFFICIAL SEX MANIACS JOKE BOOK

Larry Wilde
Illustrations by Ron Wing

BANTAM BOOKS
TORONTO · NEW YORK · LONDON · SYDNEY · AUCKLAND

THE ABSOLUTELY LAST OFFICIAL SEX MANIACS JOKE BOOK
A Bantam Book / November 1985

ISBN 0-553-25248-8

Published simultaneously in the United States and Canada

Bantam Books are published by Bantam Books, Inc. Its trade-
mark, consisting of the words ''Bantam Books'' and the por-
trayal of a rooster, is Registered in U.S. Patent and Trademark
Office and in other countries. Marca Registrada. Bantam
Books, Inc., 666 Fifth Avenue, New York, New York 10103.

PRINTED IN THE UNITED STATES OF AMERICA

O   0 9 8 7 6 5 4 3 2 1

For Jeremy Krispian—
Absolutely the last
of the great
sex maniacs.

Contents

Sexualis Satisfactus

Why is sex like a game of bridge?
If you have a good hand, you don't
need a partner.

* * *

How is Rubik's Cube like a man?
The more you play with 'em the harder
they get.

* * *

Blanche arrived home from her date on a cloud. She tossed her coat over a chair, her purse over the banister; she threw the rest of her clothing around her bedroom.

The next morning at breakfast her mother asked if she had a good time.

"Oh," sighed Blanche, "I had a wonderful time."

"I guess you did," said her mother. "Your panties are still stuck to the ceiling."

* * *

Miss Lopez, on the witness stand, was asked by the prosecutor whether or not she had screamed for help while being raped. "Yes, I did," she stated.

"And did anyone come?" asked the prosecutor.

The victim paused, then replied, "Jes, I did first. Then he did."

* * *

Why did Ronald McDonald get busted?
For stuffing his Big Mac in Wendy's Hot and Juicy.
(He knows where the beef is.

* * *

NYMPHOMANIAC

*A girl who believes that it's
every man for herself.*

* * *

What do you call a woman from Georgia who's on the pill?
A safe cracker.

* * *

Claudia and her convent-raised young daughter were riding in a taxi one evening, through an area in midtown Manhattan notorious for prostitutes.

"What are those women waiting for, Mother?" inquired the girl.

"They're probably meeting their husbands there after work," replied Claudia.

"Aw, c'mon, lady," grumbled the cab driver. "Why don'cha tell her the truth? She's old enough."

"Please, Mom," said the girl. "I want to know."

Looking daggers at the back of the driver's head, Claudia carefully explained the situation. When she finished the daughter asked, "But what happens to the babies those women have?"

"They grow up," Claudia whispered loudly, "and become taxi drivers."

3

Have you heard about the new designer rubbers?

They're made by Sergio Prevente.

*   *   *

On impulse, Grabowski stopped at the flower shop and bought a dozen roses for his girlfriend. When he handed them to her, she immediately pulled off all her clothes and leaped onto the couch. "This will be for the flowers," she announced, stretching out enticingly.

"Oh, come now," said the Polack. "Surely you got a vase somewhere in this apartment."

*   *   *

PYLON

*What a nymphomaniac might
say at a nude beach party.*

*   *   *

How can you tell if your girlfriend is too fat?

If she sits on your face and you can't hear the stereo.

*   *   *

4

Reporter:	Okay, Tarzan, I know you were born in the jungle, so you only have one name. But what's your son's name?
Tarzan:	Son's name Boy.
Reporter:	Okay, but your wife is from England. What's her name?
Tarzan:	Wife's name Jane.
Reporter:	I mean, what's Jane's whole name?
Tarzan:	Jane's whole name Pussy!

*   *   *

Fernando and Stanislaw had been drinking beer all night in a Buffalo bar. "Do you know how many tail feathers a red-headed woodpecker has?" asked Stanislaw.

"Naw," replied the Puerto Rican.

"Well," continued the Polack, "do you know how many stripes a bumblebee has on its back?"

"Naw," answered Fernando.

"Say," asked Stanislaw, "do you know how many lives a cat has?"

"Sure," replied the Puerto Rican, "nine."

"How come," demanded the Polack, "you don't know nothin' about birds and bees but you know so much about pussy?"

*   *   *

Suzanne ran up to the big, handsome Santa Monica lifeguard, thrust out her chest, fluttered her eyes, and asked, "Are topless suits allowed on this beach?"

The guard replied, "No ma'am, you've gotta keep your falsies covered."

Suzanne gulped, "How could you tell I was wearing falsies?"

"That's easy," he said. "Your tits are too big to be true; your tits are too firm to be true; your tits are too round to be true; and one of your tits is lying on the sand behind you!"

LAP DOG

A homely girl who gives head.

*　　*　　*

What's the difference between a squirrel and a man?

A squirrel puts his nuts on a rock and cracks them.

A man puts his nuts in a crack and rocks them.

*　　*　　*

Claudine, magnificently naked, smiled at a man, also exposed. "This is your first visit to a nudist colony, isn't it?" she asked.

"Why, yes it is," admitted the new member. "What gave me away, my pale complexion?"

"No," said the girl. "It's the way you can't stop pointing."

*　　*　　*

What is a coward?

That's a fellow who wakes up in the middle of the night with his nose in his girl's armpit and is afraid to open his eyes.

*　　*　　*

Will crossing a turtle with a tomcat produce a snapping pussy?

*   *   *

Did you hear about the nymphomaniac who just hated to be stood up?

*   *   *

Mrs. Dempsey and Mrs. Gilligan were chatting over the back fence. "Say," said Mrs. D., "they tell me your man Patrick has a tool so big he can make ye break wind."

"And that he can," replied Mrs. Gilligan.

"I'll be bettin' ye ten dollars he can't make me break wind," countered Mrs. D.

"And I'll be takin' that bet," retorted Mrs. G.

Arrangements were made and Patrick was called upon. He pulled out his formidable weapon, entered Mrs. Dempsey and, when halfway through, she gave out with a loud explosion of gas.

When they were finished, she said to Mrs. Gilligan, "And I'll bet ye twenty dollars that he can't do it again."

"Go on with ye," said the Irish woman. "I've a little gas on me own stomach!"

*   *   *

What's all white, and has a black asshole?
The A-Team.

* * *

Eunice and Frank were marooned on a small island in the middle of the ocean, the only two survivors of a shipwreck. Eunice was a virgin and a strict Catholic, but after a couple of months, Frank convinced her that they were never going to be rescued. Eunice finally relented and gave up her virginity.

After two years, Eunice became so ashamed of what she was doing that she killed herself.

A couple of years after she died, Frank became so ashamed of what he was doing that he buried her.

* * *

THINGS YOU SELDOM SEE

1. Horse manure in an automobile garage.
2. A man parking with his wife on a country lane.
3. A virgin with a steady job.

* * *

What do a virgin and a sneeze have in common?

It goes in tight.

*　　*　　*

Did you hear about the pro footballer who was engaged to a beautiful contortionist—until she broke it off?

*　　*　　*

Millard was fishing off the creek bank when he noticed another angler stirring the water with his pole. He hollered, "Hey, Mister, are you trying to screw up my fishin'?"

"Hell no?" answered the other man. "My gal fell in the water, and I'm trying to fish up my screwin'!"

*　　*　　*

Disney Studios is making its first X-rated movie. It's about Mickey Mouse screwing Tinkerbell, and the title will be *Little Mouse on the Fairy*.

*　　*　　*

Wylie, a 240-pound, six-foot-four construction worker, visited a bar every day after work. One day he walked into the saloon and all the regulars were shocked at his appearance. His head was shrunken to the size of a small apple.

"What happened to you?" asked the bartender.

"Well," he explained, "I found this little lamp on the construction site and when I rubbed it, this foxy genie popped out and granted me three wishes. First, I asked for a four-wheel pickup. And she gave it to me. Then I asked for a million bucks in cash. And she laid it right in my hands. Then I asked if she would give me a little head."

What is six inches long, drives a woman crazy, and has a bald head on it?

A hundred-dollar bill.

*   *   *

NYMPHOMANIA

A disease in which the patient enjoys being bedridden.

*   *   *

Miss Kowalski was suing the defendant for fathering her child. As she sat in the witness chair, the attorney asked, "And just what was the extent of the defendant's amorous involvement?"

"Well, from what I could see," replied the pretty Polish girl, "I'd say seven inches, tops."

*   *   *

Why don't chickens wear Fruit of the Loom underwear?

'Cause, silly, their peckers are on their faces.

*   *   *

Durward, a slightly built bank teller, sat in Dr. Walker's office complaining, "We live near the docks, and I don't get home from the job until after the longshoremen have quit for the day. After twice a week, I'll come home and find my wife in bed with one of those big, husky brutes, and if I try to throw him out, he'll just say something smart like, 'Well, blow me down,' and then he'll laugh at me."

"Mister Durward," interrupted the M.D., "you're in the wrong office. You don't want a medical man, you want a lawyer."

"Oh, no, I want a doctor," said Durward. "I'm afraid all that oral sex is turning me into a homosexual!"

*　　*　　*

What do you get when you cross M&Ms with a rooster?

A cock that melts in your mouth, but not in your hand.

*　　*　　*

Why is a cucumber better than a man?
Because a cucumber stays hard for a week.

*　　*　　*

Schwartz and Levine were manufacturers of prophylactic rubbers. They wanted to expand their business and tried to place an advertisement in one of the better magazines. They were turned down cold on their fancy copy extolling the virtues of their condoms. Schwartz was depressed but Levine wouldn't give up. He burst into the office one morning all smiles.

"I've got our ad all ready for the *Reader's Digest* and not once did I mention a condom," Levine announced.

"Listen," said Schwartz, "if you don't mention what we're selling, what the hell good is the ad?"

"Look," insisted Levine smiling and handing him the copy.

IF YOU WANT TO HAVE BABIES—
THAT'S YOUR BUSINESS
IF YOU DON'T—THAT'S
OUR BUSINESS.
SCHWARTZ AND LEVINE—HIGH
GRADE RUBBER GOODS

*　　*　　*

Did you hear about the flight attendant who says she has sex insomnia?
Just can't keep her thighs closed.

*　　*　　*

16

WET DREAM

Coming unscrewed.

*　　*　　*

Rayburn the funeral director was training his only child Clarissa to take over the business. One night he told her, "Come with me to the hotel. There's a nude man there, dead, and I want you to practice putting his clothes on in the dark."

Clarissa managed to get the man's jacket and shirt on all right, then said, "Daddy, it's up, and I can't get his pants zipped."

The mortician suggested, "Put your hand over the head. Sometimes that'll make 'em go down."

There was silence for awhile, then the undertaker asked, "What happened?"

The girl whispered, "You'd better wait in the hall, Daddy, I think we're in the wrong room!"

*　　*　　*

What do women and airplanes have in common?

Cockpits.

*　　*　　*

Pauline worked in the San Francisco financial district. She was very fond of fruit and, each evening while waiting for her cable car, she bought a small amount to take home. This evening, she had just picked up three bananas and, as her car was coming, paid for them, and shoved them in the lining of the jacket she was wearing.

The cable car was jammed and she had to stand. The ride was bumpy and the bananas worked around a bit. The next stop of the car was violent. It threw Pauline against the passenger next to her and she could feel one of the bananas squash.

The next stop mashed another and, thinking to salvage the third one, she reached to the back of her coat and grabbed it firmly. They rode along for a number of blocks without incident. The car stopped and the man in back of Pauline tapped her on the shoulder.

"Pardon me, Miss," he said, "but you'll have to let go now. I get off here!"

Walton was talking to his daughter and he asked, "Do you know the difference between a man and a shower?"

She thought for a minute and then said, "I dunno."

"Well," he said, "you better find out before you get under one."

* * *

Bonnie acquired Niles at a singles' bar on Friday night. Later, in bed, she remarked, "I have the strangest feeling that we've done this before."

"So do I," agreed Niles. "It's a phenomenon known as *deja blew*."

* * *

One brick said to the other, "It looks like we're going to get laid. Here comes a man with a hod on!"

* * *

PUSSYFOOT

A twelve inch peter.

* * *

CONTRACEPTIVE

An article to be worn on
every conceivable occasion.

*   *   *

Did you hear about the Eskimo who rubbed noses so indiscriminately that he contracted snyphilis?

*   *   *

Norene, a pretty cocktail waitress, went to the doctor and complained, "My vibrator is stuck up in my vagina."

"Let me take a look," said the M.D.

After the examination he said, "I've got good news and bad news."

"What is it?" asked the girl.

"The bad news is: I can't get it out. The good news is: I put a new battery in!"

*   *   *

What did the elephant say to the naked man?

How do you breathe through that little thing?

*   *   *

What do you call a Polack with 100 lovers?

A shepherd.

*   *   *

In the Old West, Miss Longbrook, a sour-faced schoolmarm, got on a train and found that the only available seat was next to a tall, bearded man dressed all in black. She took it.

After a while she spoke. "Excuse me," she said, "are you a Mormon?"

"Yes, madam," replied the man. "I am."

"Are you married?" asked Miss Longbrook.

"Yes, madam. I've got four wonderful wives," said the Mormon.

"My goodness," exclaimed the woman. "You should be hung."

"I am, madam, I am," he answered back.

*   *   *

Why do Puerto Ricans like tilted steering wheels?

More head room.

*   *   *

The dark balcony of the porno theater was practically deserted. Lisa and Jeff embraced so passionately that his toupee slid from his head. Groping to find it in the darkness, he reached under his date's skirt.

"That's it, that's it!" she gasped.

"It can't be," said Jeff. "I part mine on the side."

* * *

A waitress who lives in Palm Springs
Had her maidenhead ripped into strings
  By the biker Jack James
  And so now, she claims,
"When the wind blows through it,
  it sings."

* * *

Did you ever hear about the village smithy who made his living selling iron chastity belts at $40 a crack?

* * *

NYMPHOMANIAC

*A girl who will trip you and
get under you before you fall.*

* * *

23

Jarvis consulted a psychiatrist about his nymphomaniac girlfriend. "Doctor," he exclaimed in a shaky voice, "she'll stop at nothing to satisfy her bizarre sexual desires and weird cravings. . . ."

"I've heard enough," interrupted the shrink. "Does she have a friend?"

* * *

What did one belly button say to another belly button?

"You know, every time we get together, somebody comes!"

* * *

Emilio was having a dacquiri with his neighbor Luis in a Miami bar. "You had your blinds up last night," said Emilio, "and I saw your wife going down on you!"

Luis began laughing uncontrollably and finally said, "The joke's on you, Señor. I wasn't even home last night."

* * *

Did you hear about the Eskimo girl who spent the night with her boyfriend and next morning found she was six months pregnant?

* * *

Whit: Do you get much on the side?
Owen: It's been so long—is that where it
          is now?

*   *   *

One summer morning at a South Carolina beach, Orville tried to sell Thetchel a ticket for the annual Wetumka Turkey Raffle. Thetchel refused to buy it because he never won anything. "That's because you got no system," said Orville. "You should look for some kind of lucky sign, and then ask for that number."

Thetchel looked around and saw a big, fat, bare-bottomed woman bending over, and she had a number 7 tattooed on each cheek of her fanny. "That's surely a sign," thought Thetchel, and he bought number 77.

When raffle day rolled around, Thetchel was in bed with the flu so he phoned Orville to see if his lucky sign worked. "Your sign was correct," said Orville, "but you forgot to read between the lines. The winning ticket was 707."

*   *   *

Do you know what Jell-O is?
Kool-aid with a hard on.

*   *   *

Terry Haehl, Gualala's super Sea View Travel prexy, tittilates clients with this tall tale:

Miss Blake, a frustrated young Milwaukee schoolteacher, made her first visit to Las Vegas, and readily succumbed to the advances of the first man she met . . . a bellboy.

Following their frenzied lovemaking, she breathed in his ear, "Wouldn't it be more discreet if you got me a room where the door would stay closed?"

"Yes, ma'am," he said. "But this isn't your room, it's the elevator."

VASELINE

Penis Butter.

*   *   *

What goes in long and stiff, and comes out soft and sticky?
Chewing gum.

*   *   *

Tobias, the sex-shop owner, looked over the customer and asked, "Just what is it you intend to do with this artificial vagina, sir?"

"Listen," snapped the customer, "I really don't think that's any of your business!"

"All right, I'm just trying to be helpful," answered Tobias. "I don't have to charge you sales tax if it's a food item."

*   *   *

A Bostonian Deb named Miss Doves
Likes to jack off the athletes she loves.
   She will use her bare fist
   If the fellows insist,
But she really prefers to wear gloves.

*   *   *

As he parked the car on a secluded road, Mitch said to his girl, "When I get this incredible urge to kiss you, my teeth start chattering."

"I know just what you mean," said the pretty flight attendant, "because right now, my knees are knocking!"

*   *   *

With Robert, her boyfriend, Miss Cobb
Would nod when engaged in a job.
  It was wrongfully said
  She was bobbing her head
When she was really heading her Bob.

*   *   *

When Helga the Swedish maid came home from her first date, Dalton her employer asked if she had a good time. "Yah, sure," she replied. "First he takes me for a drive, den ve park in the woods. Den he takes from his britches a goose's neck, and he slips it in my vater hole."

Dalton said, "Now, Helga, don't go spreading that around, or the tale will be in everyone's mouth."

Helga replied, "Oh, no, sir, he put it back in his britches . . . and anyway, it didn't taste so goot like yours."

*   *   *

Have you heard about the tourist who didn't have $40 to see the Broadway musical *CATS*—and so he had to settle for some off-Broadway pussy for $25?

*   *   *

Despite his being deaf, Odgen had won the love of a simply beautiful model and married her. After they checked into their honeymoon hotel he told her, "If you wake up during the night while we're on our honeymoon and want to have sex, just reach over and pull on my organ once or twice. On the other hand," he added, "if you don't feel like having sex, pull on it 40 or 50 times."

Animalis Anecdotus

A rooster, while strutting around the barnyard early one Easter Sunday morning, came across a nest of brightly colored eggs. He cocked his head, thought a while . . . then made a beeline across the barnyard and beat hell out of the peacock.

* * *

Two buxom hens were relaxing in the farmer's pasture when suddenly one looked over her shoulder and cried, "Better move away from me, Mary. The cross-eyed rooster is around and we don't want him to come charging and miss us both again."

* * *

An old hen was walking down the road when she was hit from behind by a truck. She got up, shook her feathers, and snapped, "You don't have to be so rough!"

* * *

It wasn't the hen or the egg that came first—it was the rooster.

* * *

In the hills of Kentucky there were two little brothers, Dewey and Cloyd, aged five and seven. One day they were playing in the chicken house, when all of a sudden Dewey dashed out and went running to his mother, crying his eyes out. She picked him up and asked, "What's wrong, son?"

Dewey sobbed, "Cloyd's doing it to an ol' chicken hen, and he won't help me catch one!"

* * *

What do you get when you cross a rooster with a lion?

A cock you wouldn't believe.

*   *   *

Why do whales have more fun?

Because they have 24-inch tongues and breathe through the backs of their heads.

*   *   *

What do the president of Tupperware and a walrus have in common?

They both like a tight seal.

*   *   *

"Who has the most fun?"

"Rabbits have the most fun."

"Why do they have the most fun?"

"Because there are more of them."

"Why are there more of them?"

"Because they have the most fun!"

*   *   *

Why don't bunnies make noise when they screw?

They have cotton balls.

*   *   *

TAXIDERMIST

One who mounts animals.

* * *

Did you hear about the porcupine that bent his quill?
He tried to overpower a wire brush in a dark corner.

* * *

Here's to old King Montezuma,
For fun he would bugger a puma.
    The puma in play
    Clawed both balls away—
How's that for animal humor?

* * *

What differences are there among the grocery mouse, the laundry mouse, and the hardware mouse?
The grocery mouse sits on the cabbages and peas. The laundry mouse sits on the pillows and sheets. The hardware mouse sits on the nuts and screws.

* * *

Two mice were chatting in a laboratory.

"And how are you getting on with your professor?" one asked.

"Fine," replied the second. "I've got him so trained that every time I ring the bell, he gives me food."

*   *   *

How many mice does it take to screw in a light bulb?

Two, if they're small enough.

*   *   *

What happened to the sex-crazed mouse?

Pussy got him!

*   *   *

Why do mice have such small balls?

Because it's hard to find mice who can dance.

*   *   *

NERVIEST THING IN THE WORLD

A mouse crawling up an elephant's hind leg with intent to rape.

*   *   *

At the local zoo, Booth turned to Osgood and said, "I bet I could make that elephant jump fifteen feet in the air and shake his head 'no.' "

"I've got twenty bucks that says you can't," answered Osgood.

Booth picked up two bricks, walked around behind the elephant, and slammed them together on his jollies. Up went the elephant fifteen feet in the air.

"That's great!" exclaimed Osgood. "But let's see you make him shake his head 'no.' "

So Booth walked around in front of the elephant, held up the bricks and asked, "Want me to do it again?"

You know what a barroom is, don't you?

That's when an elephant farts in an open elevator shaft—barrooooom!!!

*   *   *

The census taker arrived at a West Virginia hill dwelling and knocked on the door. Little Billy opened it.

"Where's your mother, sonny?" said the man.

"Out in back with the goat," said the child.

The census taker couldn't believe it. The boy led him around to the back of the house where he discovered the woman getting it on with the goat.

"Doesn't that bother you, kid?" asked the man.

"Naaaaaaaaaaah!" said the kid.

*   *   *

All animals talk—if only we knew how to listen:

One male elephant to another male elephant as a female passes: "Wow—a perfect 320–350–365!"

*   *   *

Berkowitz got all dressed up in fancy riding clothes, rented a horse from a riding stable, and went for a canter in Central Park. After being out for several hours he returned to the stable.

"I should like," he stated, "to reserve this same stallion for tomorrow."

"Say what?" exclaimed the attendant. "That ain't no stallion. We don't have no stallion in the entire stable. What gave you that idea?"

"Well," said Berkowitz, "as I rode along today, I heard several people say, 'Hey, look at the big prick on that horse!' "

*   *   *

Did you hear about the flea that had insomnia?

He had to sleep in snatches.

*   *   *

A bloody-nosed, badly ruffled squirrel lay gasping for breath at the foot of a tall elm.

"What happened to you?" inquired a passing chipmunk.

"Wanna know something?" gasped the squirrel. "This mating in the treetops—that's for the birds."

*   *   *

The active days were over for old Basil the bull but kindly farmer Sheffield permitted him to stay on in the pasture with the cows. Of course Sheffield also turned a young bull loose in the field, and the newcomer went to work immediately. Seeing this, old Basil began snorting and pawing the ground with his hoof.

"You're wasting your time," said the farmer. "You're too old for that sort of thing now."

"I know," said the bull. "But I can show him I'm not a cow, can't I?"

*   *   *

Said a cow in the pasture, "My dear,
Don't count on much romance 'round here.
  I start with high hopes
  But they come up with dopes—
And I end with the usual bum steer."

*   *   *

Did you hear about the talkative bull?
Every time he saw a cow he wanted to jabber.

*   *   *

Two jet planes flew plast two crows.

"They were really going, weren't they?" said the first crow.

The second crow said, "You'd be going too if if you had two assholes and they were both on fire!"

* * *

Then there was the fickle cow that switched her tail.

* * *

Why was Ferdinand late for the bull fight?

He found the hole in his Jersey.

* * *

During a wild party at a photographer's country place, an attractive Vegas showgirl strolled outdoors for some air. In a grassy field nearby, she lay down to watch the stars.

She was almost asleep when a cow, searching for clover, carefully stepped over her. Groggily, she raised her head and murmured, "One at a time, boys. One at a time."

* * *

Barton's favorite cow suddenly stopped giving milk. The farmer tried everything. Better grass. Sweeter hay. Nothing helped.

"My Bessie used to give the thickest milk with the most butter fat of any cow around here," Barton complained to a neighbor. "Now she don't give nothin'."

"Why don't you take her to one of them psychiatrist fellers," suggested the other farmer.

"They got 'em for animals, too?"

"Why sure!" the second assured.

Barton brought Bessie into town and sought out an animal psychiatrist. When they entered Dr. Crawford's office the M.D. said, "Now you just sit out here in the waiting room while I examine your cow."

Twenty minutes later, Barton noticed a trickle of milk coming out from under the office door. Then it turned into a flood. Soon the shrink opened the door and led Bessie out. She was swinging her tail, and had a big smile on her face.

"Say, she looks wonderful," said the farmer. "What'd you do to her?"

"You're just like the rest of these guys," said the doc. "You pat 'em on the ass, pull on their tits, and never tell 'em you love 'em."

CASTRATED DINOSAUR

*A colossal fossil with a
docile tassle.*

* * *

Chambley, a handsome Australian, arrived in San Diego and very soon met Nessa, a pretty secretary. She invited him up to her apartment.

When the girl removed her blouse, Chambley threw a chair out the window. Nessa then took off her skirt, whereupon Chambley threw a table out the window.

"Say, fella," shouted the girl, "do you have any idea what we're going to do?"

"I think I do, m'am," said the Aussie. "If it's anything like it is with a kangaroo we're gonna need all the room we can get."

* * *

A nuisance and pest is a rabbit.
When he spies your best lettuce he'll grab it.
  He doesn't rate high
  In brains, but oh my!
He surely knows how to cohabit!

* * *

44

What makes a bull sweat?
A tight Jersey.

*　　*　　*

Throat specialist Winters was duck hunting with urologist Baxter early one morning while it was still dark. They heard an owl in a tree above them snoring.

"I'm such a great surgeon," bragged Winters, "I'm gonna go up there and remove that owl's tonsils without even waking him."

Ten minutes later the throat specialist returned showing his medical pal the two teeny nodes.

"Hell," said the urologist, "I'm so deft with my hands I'll go up there and remove that bird's testicles without his even knowing it."

Five minutes later, Baxter returned holding the bird's tiny little balls.

Three months passed. The owl was flying over the same tree with a buddy. "Hey," said his friend, "let's sleep down there tonight!"

"No way," exclaimed the owl. "I slept down there three months ago and ever since I haven't been able to screw worth a hoot or hoot worth a screw!"

*　　*　　*

*   *   *

Did you hear about the lark that eloped with a woodpecker, and learned that love is a many-splintered thing?

*   *   *

The leopard and the zebra wed,
The reason . . . who could know?
But from their striped and spotted bed
Came a baby tic-tac-toe!

*   *   *

What do you get when you cross an ant eater with a vibrator?
An Armadildo.

*   *   *

A huge Texas bird, mean and tough as nails, wanted to get laid. It leaped on a lark who went off tweeting, "I'm a lark and I've been sparked!" Then on a dove who cooed, "I'm a dove and I've been loved."

Then a duck came by and, after a good deal of commotion and flying feathers, the duck waddled away muttering, "I'm a drake, and there's been a mistake."

*   *   *

*   *   *

As the possum said while making love to the pole cat, "I've enjoyed about as much of this as I can stand. . . ."

*   *   *

What's green and smells like pork? Kermit's finger.

*   *   *

Farmer Coggin complained to the vet that his stock was not breeding. "Don't worry," said the vet. "I'll make up a sack of stuff that'll get them going. Send your man for it."

The farmer dispatched Zepticki, his hired hand. On his way back, the fellow carelessly ripped the sack on some wire and the stuff trailed across the fields.

That evening Zepticki rushed in to the farm house and shouted, "Boss, the goat's doing the sow, the cock's doing the ducks, the bull's doing the mare. . . ."

"Don't stand there like a fool—get out and throw some cold water over them!" screamed the farmer.

"I can't. The donkey's doing the pump."

*   *   *

Mrs. Harris stood before the chimpanzee cage and watched in frozen horror. One of the chimps picked up a peanut and placed it in his rectum, then pulled it out and ate it.

The chimp took another peanut, put it in his ass, pulled it out and ate it. The distraught woman rushed over to the zookeeper and said, "I thought chimpanzees were supposed to be the most intelligent animal next to man."

"That's right, lady," said the zookeeper.

"Then why is he doing that disgusting thing?" she countered.

"Well, some boy scouts were here yesterday and gave him peaches to eat. He had trouble passing the pits. Now he checks everything for size."

There once was a sacred baboon
That lived by the river Rangoon,
   And all of the women
   That came to go swimmin'
He'd bang by the light of the moon.

*   *   *

When Noah took the animals on the Ark, in order to keep them from fighting and catting around, he issued each of the males a claim check, and made them leave their privates at the door.

On the night before they landed, the boy monkey eased over to the girl monkey and whispered, "There's gonna be hot times tomorrow, baby. I stole the elephant's ticket stub!"

*   *   *

HORSE SHOW

*A lot of horses showing their asses
to a lot of horses' asses showing
their horses.*

*   *   *

Did you hear about the nearsighted skunk?

He tried to rape a fart.

*   *   *

THRIFTY TOMCAT

One that puts a little in
the kitty every night.

*   *   *

Did you hear about the new ball-bearing mousetrap on the market?

It's called a Tomcat.

*   *   *

Manny, Moe, and Jack, three mice, were in a bar doing some heavy drinking. Soon they became thoroughly drunk and each began to boast about his bravery. I'm going to tell off that Reagan in the White House about some of his dumb politics,'' said Manny.

''That's nothing,'' sneered Moe. ''I'm going over to the Kremlin and tell them just what I think of them.''

They turned to Jack who was sitting there dreaming. ''What are you going to do?'' they demanded.

''Me? I'm going to screw the cat.''

*   *   *

''They're off!'' said the monkey
when he backed into the lawnmower.

*   *   *

With all the animals safely aboard the Ark, Noah assembled them in the central cabin for a short speech. He pointed out that the trip could be a long one, and that quarters were somewhat cramped and limited.

"Therefore," he announced, "I want to emphasize that we can't have a single population increase of any kind until the flood subsides and we can get to land. I'm appointing the giraffe, since he is the tallest of you, to stand guard and see that my instructions are carried out."

At long last, the waters subsided. The Ark landed on the mountainside and the doors were flung open. Out poured the animals, two by two, just as they had entered— only one pair of each kind. But suddenly the two cats came out, followed by a litter of kittens.

As they passed the giraffe, the tomcat winked and meowed, "I'll bet you thought we were fighting!"

Femalis Fornicatus

Tania and Erica were reminiscing about their childhood. "Did you ever play with jacks?" asked Tania.

"Oh, yes," replied Erica. "And with Tommy's, Bill's, and Freddy's."

* * *

PREGNANT COWGIRL

*A chick who went on a roundup
and let her calves get spread.*

*　　*　　*

Darlene and Lenore were talking about
the handsome young stud who had just moved
into their St. Louis luxury apartment build-
ing for singles.

"He acts so stupid," said Darlene. "I
think all his brains are between his legs."

"Yeah," sighed Lenore, "and I'd love
to blow his mind."

*　　*　　*

Lawyer:　Now is this correct? You say you
were in the swimming pool of the
country club when this alleged
rape took place?
Magda:　Yes, that's correct.
Lawyer:　And you claim the defendant raped
you in the pool?
Magda:　Oh yes, in front of a lot of people.
Lawyer:　Well, why on earth didn't you
scream or yell for help?
Magda:　I was afraid he'd duck me.

*　　*　　*

After he entered a packed subway train, Stanton was crushed up against a shapely Puerto Rican girl. Several stations later, as he started to get off, she kicked him in the shin. "What the hell did you do that for?" he asked.

"Next time," whispered the girl, "don't start something you can't finish."

* * *

What's a macho woman?

She starts her own vibrator and rolls her own tampons.

* * *

When Marna, the young career girl, consulted Doctor Coulter about her diminishing sexuality, he gave her a hormone shot. "Call me in a week," he advised.

Seven days later, Marna wailed over the phone, "My voice has become terribly low."

"That's not too unusual," replied the physician. "Have you had any other reactions?"

"Yes," she moaned. "I've sprouted hair on my chest."

"My goodness," gasped the M.D. "How far down does it go?"

"All the way to my testicles."

Priscilla and Rip tossed and scuffled on the bed in ecstacy for almost three hours. Finally, they were spent and they lay back for the moment, exhausted. Rip reached for his cigarettes and, holding the pack out to Priscilla he asked, "Do you smoke?"

"I don't know," she replied. "Let me look."

Said Luberta on one of her larks,
"It's better in bed than in parks.
    You feel more at ease,
    Your fanny don't freeze,
And crude passers don't make snide
remarks."

*   *   *

Evita and Rosa were chatting at a coffee break. "Do you shave between your legs?" asked Evita.

"Why should I?" replied Rosa. "No man minds going through a little brush to get to a picnic."

*   *   *

"I'd like you to kiss me," she said.
"Between my toes, please bend your head.
    No, not there, oh no!
    It tickles me so. . . .
Between the two big ones instead."

*   *   *

HUMDINGER

A girl who hums
every time she sees a dinger.

*   *   *

Flanders, a young zoologist, entered a Baltimore lounge and ordered a triple martini. He proudly told the bartender that he was celebrating his first major achievement in the field of genetics. Justine, a pretty housewife at the other end of the bar, asked if she might join him. "I'm celebrating an outstanding personal accomplishment, too."

"What a coincidence," said the zoologist. "I've just succeeded in breeding a very rare, blue-eyed, female pheasant for the first time in captivity. What did you do?"

"Nothing quite so significant," replied the woman. "It's just that after ten years of marriage, I'm finally pregnant. . . . But how did you ever manage to breed your blue-eyed pheasant?"

"It was simple," he explained. "All I did was keep changing mates until I found the right biological combination."

"Really?" said the girl. "That *is* a coincidence!"

* * *

Isabel: I have the autographs of 69 movie stars!
Joanna: So what, I've got more than that.
Isabel: On your diaphragm?

* * *

The phone rang in the Pittsburgh apartment of Phyllis, a pretty flight attendant.

"Hello, darling," breathed the obscene phone caller. "If you can guess what's in my hand, I'll give you a piece of the action!"

"Listen, shmuck," replied the girl, "if you can hold it in one hand. I'm not interested."

* * *

Malcom, a truck driver, sat on his stool in the Nashville restaurant eye-balling the good-looking waitress. She wandered over, put her elbows on the counter, and leaned over, revealing two magnificently ripe melons.

"Would you care for anything else?" she asked.

"Yes, I would," said Malcolm. "I'd like a little pussy."

"Gollee!" she exclaimed. "So would I. Mine's a great big thing!"

* * *

Sir Lancelot had been complaining about the fit for quite some time. Finally, the queen went secretly to a famous plastic surgeon for a general genital tightening. "And now," she mused happily, "I'm all tucked in for the knight."

*   *   *

Wiley: I'd sure like to get in your pants.
Sibyl: Why? There's already one ass in
        'em.

*   *   *

"Take your glasses off," the girl demanded. "They're tearing my stockings!"

A few seconds later she giggled and said, "Better put them back on, you're kissing the shag rug!"

*   *   *

Portia and Edwina, two violinists, were having drinks around the corner from Carnegie Hall at The Russian Tea Room. "I hear you dated the new conductor," said Portia.

"Yes, I did," answered Edwina.

"How was he?"

"Disappointing."

"But they say he has a dong as long as his baton," declared Portia.

"That's true."

"Well, why was it disappointing?"

"Let me put it this way. He can't conduct either."

*   *   *

61

Parker Johnson, Santa Rosa's popular Volvo Service Manager, treats customers to this pleasant snip of persiflage:

After a wild chase on a California freeway, the motorcycle cop pulled the speeding sports car over to the shoulder.

When Officer Koch walked up to the driver's window, he was surprised to find a beautiful blonde behind the wheel. "Ma'am," he said, "I'm afraid we're going to have to give you a Breathalyzer test to see whether or not you've been drinking."

The test was taken and as the policeman eyed the results. He said, "Lady, you've had a couple of stiff ones."

"That's amazing!" said the blonde. "You mean it shows that, too?"

Did you hear about the modern Cinderella who turns into a motel every night?

* * *

There was a young Texan named Biddle
Whose girl had to teach him to fiddle.
   She grabbed hold of his bow
   And said, "If you want to know,
You can try parting my hair in the middle."

* * *

Pandora got a pair of panties tattooed on her for only $10. So her friend Sally went and asked the price of tattooing a brassiere on her. The tattoo artist quoted her $50.

"How come my friend got a pair of panties tattooed for only $10?" asked Sally.

"Because I went in the hole on that deal," admitted the tattooer.

"In that case," snapped Sally, "how about taking a licking on this deal?"

* * *

Did you hear about the southern gal who put zip codes on her stomach so the male could come faster?

* * *

The teenage Valley Girl bounced into a Sherman Oaks card shop. "Do you have any, like, real special valentines?" she asked.

"Here's one from our private line," smirked the salesman as he slipped it out from under the counter. "It's inscribed, 'To the Boy Who Got My Cherry'!"

"Like wow!" burbled the girl. "I'll take the whole box."

* * *

Thrope: You look sexier every minute we drive! You know what that's a sign of?

Nessa: You're going to run out of gas.

* * *

Hester and Lottie were sitting on a Santa Monica beach having a gab session about sex. Hester said, "It's been my experience that some male organs have a fishy taste."

"I can live with fishiness," said Lottie, "but what I can't tolerate is shrimpiness."

* * *

What do you call lint on a sanitary napkin?
Cliti litter.

* * *

Phoebe charged up to the nudist camp director and exclaimed, "I have a complaint, Mr. Croft!"

"Yes?" asked the director. "What is it?"

"I want to report that the new member, Gloria Bleeker, is breaking the rules by covering herself indecently, over in the willow grove."

"Well, Phoebe," asked Croft, "just what is she covering herself indecently with?"

"My boyfriend!" screeched the girl.

Did you hear about the fun-loving Toledo girl who insists she won't even consider marriage until she's gotten some experience under her belt?

* * *

Andrea listened patiently as her married sister raved about the benefits of the quiet life. "That's not for me," she announced. "I once tried to give up drinking, smoking, and sex—and it was the longest twenty minutes I ever spent."

* * *

Felice: I wonder what girls did in the evening years ago when there was no T.V.?

Glenna: The same thing they do today— but without T.V.

* * *

During the frantic rush hour on a New York subway train, a lecherous old man pressed up close to Louise and whispered in her ear, "You know, you're rather a tasty morsel."

"And do you know," she snapped, "that it's impolite to eat with your hands?"

* * *

Blanche and Ilsa, two Seattle house-wives, were having lunch when Blanche noticed that something was bothering her friend.

"Out with it," she commanded. "What's depressing you so?"

"I'm ashamed to admit it," moaned Ilsa, "but I caught my husband making love."

"Why let that bother you?" laughed Blanche. "I got mine the same way."

*   *   *

"I don't have to chase you," said Yves. "Remember, there are plenty more fish in the sea."

"That's true," agreed Cher. "But you'll never catch any with the bait you've shown me."

*   *   *

"What's your name?"

"Tyrone Welch, but you can call me Ty. What's your name?"

"Vicki Dale, but you can call me anytime."

*   *   *

MANHATTAN MELODRAMA

PLACE: *A small boozery on upper Broadway.*

TIME: *Nine-thirty, any evening.*

ACTION: *A young Puerto Rican couple enter, look around, and cross to a small booth.*

DIALOGUE:

Ramon: What would you like?

Silvia: You know what I'd like, but let's have a drink first.

* * *

Norman, the town bachelor, went off and married Tricia, a big-city girl. She was spoiling his homecoming party by being uppity and snooty to all the girls, but she finally met her match.

One of the prettiest girls in town walked up to her and said, "So you're Norman's bride! We're all so happy he finally found someone who would do it his way!"

* * *

Tina: Are that guy's pants torn or am I seeing things?

June: Both.

* * *

*   *   *

Enrique and Ynes arrived at their Pennsylvania honeymoon hotel. The nervous groom became worried about the state of his bride's innocence. Deciding on a direct approach, he quickly undressed, pointed at his exposed manhood and asked his mate, "Do you know what that is?"

Her face turned red but Ynes replied, "That's a wee-wee."

Thrilled with the thought of showing his naive wife the ways of love, the Puerto Rican whispered, "From now on, baby, this is gonna be called a prick."

"Oh, come now," said the girl. "I seen lots of pricks and believe me that's a wee-wee."

*   *   *

Charlie sat down next to Gladys, a good-looking black jack dealer at a Vegas bar, and tried to pick her up.

"Can I buy you a drink, honey?"

"Do you like sex?" she asked.

"You better believe it!"

"Do you like to travel!"

"Sure."

"Screw off!" exclaimed the girl.

*   *   *

Rosita, a housemaid, had been working at the Greenberg home for two years. One day she said, "Mrs. Greenberg, I'm pregnant and ain't got no husband. I don't know what to do."

Mrs. Greenberg, being a kindly woman, said, "Don't worry dear, have the child and I will adopt it."

A year and a half went by and the Mexican girl approached her employer, saying, "Mrs. Greenberg, I got another baby comin'!"

Her employer was annoyed but didn't want to lose Rosita's services, so she adopted the second child, too. Three months after the birth of the second baby, Rosita went to Mrs. Greenberg and said, "I sorry, lady, but I leavin'. I can't work for no lady with two children."

Old Codger

Young Cynthia had married a senior citizen and they flew to their Florida honeymoon. They checked into their Miami room, but, try as she might, the bride couldn't get the groom in condition to consummate their marriage.

Finally in desperation, she cried, "If I stand on my head, do you think you can drop it in?"

*   *   *

Astrid and Madeline, both in their early twenties, were engaged to two old codgers. Astrid got married first and started on her honeymoon. A few days later Madeline received a telegram:

IF YOU HAVEN'T DONE IT, DON'T DO IT. DID YOU EVER TRY TO DROP A RAW OYSTER IN A SLOT MACHINE?

* * *

"It's really amazing," Harriet told her rich, elderly lover as she tenderly played with him. "You have a handsome head of gray hair, and yet there isn't a touch of gray in your pubic bush."

"Why should there be?" responded the self-made tycoon. "That cock of mine has never had a worry in its life."

* * *

There was an old lecher named Gus
Who wore a horrible truss;
    It would pinch, sweat and itch,
    When the son of a bitch
Got too close to a young girls on a bus.

* * *

Did you hear about the 80-year-old man accused of rape but later acquitted because the evidence wouldn't stand up in court?

*　　*　　*

The elderly farm couple sat in their rocking chairs in front of the fireplace one wintry night in Nebraska.

"The years are passing us by, Sarah," said the old man.

"Yes," she agreed.

"We're getting older," he said, "and pretty soon only one of us will be left."

"That's right," she said, "and when that happens, I'm moving to California."

*　　*　　*

GROSS

When you kiss your grandmother goodbye and she slips you the tongue.

*　　*　　*

Perkins was informed by his doctor, "Your hearing is getting worse and you must cut out smoking, drinking, and women."

The old man replied, "What? Just so I can hear a little better?"

*　　*　　*

Cleveland police officer Dugan spotted a disturbance outside a porno theater. He went over to investigate, and found young Birdwell kicking an 80-year-old man.

Dugan started to make an arrest, but Birdwell exclaimed, "Hey, the old geezer told me to do it."

"That's true," said the octogenarian. "Many years ago, during the Great Depression, I picked up a young girl on the street who said she was starving. I took her to my apartment, and I fed her some cold chicken, salmon patties, hash brown potatoes, glazed carrots, salad and string beans, followed by chocolate cake and a half-pint of ice cream. Her stomach was full by this time, but she says to me, 'Now is there something else I can nibble on?' I was horrified by this seeming ingratitude, and chased out her of the apartment.

"As she left, she told me, 'One day you'll think about this, and you'll ask the first man you meet to kick you.'

"I just this evening found out what she meant."

The policeman turned to Birdwell and said, "Kick him again, Buddy!"

OLD AGE

*A time when a man sees a pretty
girl and it arouses his memory
instead of his hopes.*

*   *   *

On his eighty-second birthday, Udell
got a date with a beautiful secretary. They
went back to her apartment and started kissing on the sofa. The old man said to her,
"I'm going to ravish you and you are going
to yell and holler with happiness!"

Twenty minutes later, the old guy said,
"I'm going to do it to you again and this
time you're going to scream even louder!"

Thirty minutes later he turned to her
and said, "Now this time, you're going to
sweat!"

"Why," she asked, "am I going to
sweat?"

"Because," he replied, "it'll be next
August!"

*   *   *

Did you hear about the old man who
married the pretty, young airline hostess from
the neighborhood?

All his friends had it in for him.

*   *   *

*   *   *

Whitman, 86, and Zachary, 78, were sitting on a park bench. "My grandson gave me one of them RCA video recorders," announced Whitman, "and last night I watched my first X-rated movie."

"How was it?" asked Zachary.

"I was so shocked, I could hardly sit through it the third time!"

*   *   *

An inquiring reporter from the *San Francisco Chronicle* stopped a well-dressed senior citizen in the financial district and asked, "Are you against sin?"

"Of course I'm against sin," he replied. "I'm against anything I'm too old to enjoy."

*   *   *

Hollis and Elmer, two elderly Wyoming ranchers, were strolling through a pasture when Hollis stopped and said, "Here's where I got my first piece. And right over there is where her mother stood."

"Her mother!" cried Elmer.

"What did she say?"

"*Ba-a-a-a-a-a-a*," came the reply.

*   *   *

Melburn was a sprightly 88 years of age when he married Ruby, a lusciously ripe 18-year-old. As they prepared for bed on their wedding night, he asked her, "Tell me, sweet child, did your mother tell you the facts of life?"

She blushed furiously and then murmured, "No."

"That's too bad," he said, "because I'm afraid I've forgotten them."

*   *   *

Barney, aged 74, was drinking martinis at a Las Vegas hotel and cavorting around the dance floor like a 20-year-old. Finally, the waitress approached him. "S'cuse me, sir," she said. "It's amazing a gentleman your age living it up like a youngster. Are all of your faculties unimpaired?"

"Not all," said the old fellow. "Last night, I went out with a girlfriend—we drank and danced all night and finally got to her place about 2 A.M. We went right to bed and I was asleep almost as soon as my head hit the pillow. I woke around 3:30 and nudged my girl. 'Why, Barney,' she said in surprise, 'we just finished the third one 15 minutes ago.'

"So you see," said the old boy, "my memory is beginning to fail me."

*   *   *

At a Park Avenue cocktail party the old, white-haired publisher was working very hard to convince the well-stacked babe of his virility.

Turning on all the charm he purred, "There may be winter in my hair, dear, but there's summer in my heart!"

"Yes, but tell me," she responded, "is there any spring in your ass?"

* * *

Old Murdock had heard that the best way to freeze corn was in prophylactics, an ear of corn to each rubber.

On Thursday, he purchased a dozen to try them out. It worked so well that on Friday he bought two dozen more.

He decided to put more in the freezer. On Saturday he went back for another three dozen rubbers but the store was out.

"Gee," sighed the little girl that had waited on him for all of his purchases," I hope we haven't spoiled your Saturday night for you."

* * *

Said the eager gal to her aging lover, "Do you think playing "The Star Spangled Banner would help?"

* * *

An old maid in the land of Aloha
Got wrapped in the coils of a boa;
   And as the snake squeezed
   The maid, not displeased,
Cried, "Darling! I love it! Samoa!"

*   *   *

Grandpa may be too old to cut the mustard, but he can still lick the jar.

*   *   *

THE HISTORY OF SEX

At 20, you're raring to go,
At 40, you're willing but slow,
At 60, you never know when,
   At 80—never again.

*   *   *

At a New Jersey home for the aged, two residents were chatting on the porch. "Do you think there's as much sex and romance going on as there used to be?" asked one.

"I guess so," nodded the second, "except there's a new bunch doing it."

*   *   *

When a storm came up, Aunt Martha was so frightened she ran to a haystack and burrowed her head into it. The wind blew her dress over her head. Virgil, the rural mailman who was passing by, spied her and, being an opportunist of a few words, walked up behind her and made the most of the situation.

"Oh," cried the spinster. "I didn't know that lightning felt like that. Strike again, old lightning, strike again!"

*　　*　　*

Aunt Loma sat before Madame La Zonga, the famous Atlantic City gypsy fortune-teller. "I see a great loss in your life—the death of your husband, perhaps."

"But I have no husband," the spinster protested. "I've never been married."

The gypsy said, "Well, then someone will break into your house and steal all your candles."

*　　*　　*

There was an old spinster named Mead
Who was prudish in thought, word and deed,
　　Yet held it no scandal
　　To press on the handle
Of the vessel in which she wee-weed.

Officers Monroe and Fenton were cruising around looking for trouble late one night when they spied two little old ladies in the front seat of a beaten-up 1967 Chevy convertible on a used-car lot. The place was closed, so Monroe drove his patrol car up close and gently inquired, "Are you two ladies trying to steal this fine automobile?"

The woman behind the wheel waved a bill of sale and giggled, "My goodness, no, Officer. We purchased the car this afternoon."

Fenton drawled, "Then why don't you put her in gear and drive it out of here?"

The old gal twittered, "Oh, we don't drive. We were told if we bought a vehicle here, we'd get screwed!"

84

Whitcomb, Delmar and Rocklin, all in their eighties, watched a young lovely approaching.

"Gosh," said Whitcomb, "I'd sure like to take her out to dinner and the theater."

"I'd like to bite her on the ear," said Delmar.

"Well, I'd like to take her up to my room and kiss her," stated Rocklin, ". . . and what's that other thing we used to do to girls?"

* * *

Miss Prudence rushed up to the policeman. "I've been raped. I've been attacked!" she cried. "He ripped off my clothing. He smothered me with burning kisses. Then he made mad passionate love to me!"

"Take it easy, lady," said the officer. "Just when did all this take place?"

"Twenty-three years ago this September," said the old maid.

"Twenty-three years ago!" he exclaimed. "How do you expect me to arrest anyone for something he did twenty-three years ago?"

"Oh, I don't want you to arrest anyone," said the spinster. "I just like to talk about it, that's all."

* * *

THE HEIGHT OF PASSION

*Two old maids playing squat
tag in an asparagus patch.*

*   *   *

Did you hear about the old maid who
uses a pickle for self-satisfaction?
Her birth control dill.

*   *   *

Charlotte: I hate to think of my youth.
Eustacia: What happened?
Charlotte: Nothing.

*   *   *

An old maid in silk underwear is like
malted milk in a champagne bottle.

*   *   *

WALL STREET JOURNAL AD

*Fifty thousand old maids to volunteer
for a good-will tour of the Arab Oil States.
No speechmaking required, just let 'em see
what happens when you hold onto something so long nobody else wants it.*

*   *   *

"Come on in, honey," the old maid told the furtive-looking guy on the fire escape.

"No thanks," he said, "I'm just looking."

*   *   *

Auntie Cassandra was losing a lot of sleep because of a recurring dream. Finally, in desperation, she went to a psychiatrist.

"It's always the same," she blushingly told the shrink. "In this dream I'm chased by a handsome football player. Although I try my best to get away he always catches me—and makes the most violent love to me."

The doctor smiled. "Take these pills," he told the spinster. "Then come back and see me next week."

The following week Cassandra returned looking refreshed, but sad.

"The pills worked, and I slept better than I have in months," she told the doc. "But I sure miss that football player!"

*   *   *

OLD MAID

A female who said "No" once too often.

*   *   *

A spinster in Kalamazoo
Once strolled after dark by the zoo.
　　She was seized by the nape,
　　And raped by an ape,
And she murmured, "A wonderful screw."

*　　*　　*

　　Aunt Constance left a ten-dollar bill on
the bureau. A burglar came in, grabbed the
bill, kissed her, and beat it. The next night
she put a twenty-dollar bill there.

*　　*　　*

　　"How come that old spinster keeps getting the best boyfriends at the dances?"
　　"That's easy. When she was young
she gave it away. Later, she sold it and,
now that she's rich, she's buying it back."

*　　*　　*

A pious old spinster named Tweak
Had taught her vagina to speak.
　　It was frequently liable
　　To quote from the Bible,
But when screwing—not even a squeak!

*　　*　　*

Clarence Boyle, the octogenarian bawdy-story collector, breaks up buddies with this beaut:

Old man Nelson picked up Rita at the hotel bar and took her up to his room. They went to bed and she was trying to coax him into condition.

"Say, honey," he asked, "how old are you?"

"Oh," she replied, "I'm nineteen."

"My God," he cried, jumping up. "You'll have to get dressed and get out of here, you're too young!"

"Relax, pop," said Rita, "and get back in bed. By the time you're ready, I'll be old enough!"

Did you hear about the old maid who got tired of using candles, so she called the electrician?

*   *   *

Vinnie had made love to everything that could be screwed. But he heard about an old lady who had an unusual way of fornicating, so he went up and beat on the door. A 90-year-old woman answered.

"You got some way of screwing that's different?" he asked.

She said, "Yes, come in." When he got into the house, the old lady popped her eye out and said, "Put it in here."

Afterward, Vinnie said, "Not bad, I'll probably be back for more someday."

"O.K.," said the old woman, "I'll keep an eye out for you."

*   *   *

A burglar broke into a house where a little, old retired couple lived and, after robbing them, he decided to rape the old lady.

When the robber left, the old lady said, "Percy, wasn't that awful?"

The old man replied, "If it was so awful why did you wiggle?"

*   *   *

*   *   *

Grandpa: Doc, you remember that "vitality" medicine you gave me last week?
Doctor: Yes, what about it?
Grandpa: I accidently dropped it in the well.
Doctor: Goodness, man! You're not drinking the water, are you?
Grandpa: Heck, no! We can't even get the pump handle down.

*   *   *

Everett and Lottie, a North Carolina couple in their seventies, came home from their granddaughter's wedding. That night in bed they began discussing their own early days of passion. It had been at least ten years since they'd been intimate but they decided to try it again.

So, giggling and blushing, they started playing around. An hour later, they were still fooling around, and the old lady cried, "It's no use, Pa. That old log of yours just won't kindle no more!"

"Maybe not," said the old codger, "but it seems to me like your flue don't draw like it used to, neither."

*   *   *

"Has your grandfather stopped chasing women?"

"No, but we got him to slow down. We took the tires off his wheelchair."

*　　*　　*

Grandpa came for a visit with his oldest daughter and, as sleeping quarters were limited, he was forced to bunk with Kyle, his 16-year-old grandson.

In the middle of the night he woke the boy up shouting, "Get me a woman! Get me a woman! My gosh, this hasn't happened to me for years. Get me a woman!"

"Calm down, Grandpa," soothed Kyle. "What you've got in your head is yours, but what you've got in your hand is mine!"

*　　*　　*

Did you hear about the 80-year-old man who married the 20-year-old girl?

For a wedding present, he gave her a Do-It-Yourself Kit.

*　　*　　*

An old codger marrying a young girl is like buying peanut brittle when you have no teeth.

*　　*　　*

Ida, age 82, lay on her death bed. She motioned to Isadore, her 86-year-old husband, to move closer. She whispered, "I'm dying. I have one last request!"

"Anything!" he replied. "Just name it!"

"Sweetheart, go down on me just once."

The old man froze at what he had just heard. Then he threw back the covers, took out his teeth, and granted his dying wife her last wish.

When he had finished, the old woman suddenly jumped out of bed and began dancing around the room. "I'm well! Isadore, you saved my life!"

The husband began crying, and his wife asked, "Why are you weeping?"

"Just think," answered Isadore, "I could've saved my sister . . . my mother . . . Mrs. Roosevelt!"

* * *

One day Farmer Watkins decided he was getting too old to do all the work himself, so he called the employment office and asked for an elderly man to help with the chores. The lady asked, "Why not a young man? We have one in the office right now."

The farmer replied, "I want an older man because I have an old tractor and a young wife, and I don't want a rod thrown in either one of them."

Bruce McKelvey, California's premier periodontist, calms patients with this playful pearl:

Great Uncle George had lived a good life until 96 when he finally died. Several years later, Wally, his boyhood friend, joined George in heaven and found him seated on a fluffy, pink cloud, with a very pretty, young blonde at his knees.

At the sight of this touching scene Wally said, ''I'm so happy to see you've received the reward you deserve.''

''She isn't my reward,'' sighed the old man. ''I'm her punishment.''

My friend passed away at 69,
    And we'll all miss him so.
My friend passed away at 69,
    But what a way to go!

*   *   *

Old man Epstein went to a doctor and the M.D. told him he had just two days left to live. Epstein wanted to make the best of his 48 hours, so the physician gave him an unusual medicine: when he heard *Beep* his manhood would go up; with *Beep Beep*, it would go down.

Epstein left the office and, while driving home, he got caught in a traffic jam. The guy in the car behind him blew on the horn. *Beep* and up it went. Then *Beep Beep* and it went down.

Epstein arrived home, rushed into the house, grabbed his wife, ripped her clothes off and yelled, *Beep*.

His wife said, "What is this *Beep Beep* stuff?"

*   *   *

An old man who can still make love is a lucky stiff.

*   *   *

Astronauts and old men have a problem in common: re-entry.

*   *   *

How do you find an old man in a nudist colony?

It's not hard.

*   *   *

Miss Wilson, a social worker, hearing a group of refugees would be brought to a nearby church, got into her car and rushed to the spot. Soon a truck appeared laden with people.

Clinging together on the edge of the crowd were an old man and old woman.

"You two," she said. "Would you like to come home with me?"

After a quick consultation, they agreed. She took them to her house, gave them a good meal, and showed them to the guest room.

In a few moments the little old lady appeared. "Thank you for your kindness—I really 'preciate you being so nice, but would you be good enough to answer one question?"

"Of course," she said.

"Who is this old man I'm supposed to sleep with?"

*   *   *

"You know you're getting old when your back starts going out more than you do."

Whittaker, age 84, was talking to his doctor: "I've a confession to make. About four weeks ago, I picked up a 22-year-old secretary, took her to a motel, and we made love all night. Three weeks ago, I picked up a 20-year-old nurse, parked in front of her house, and made love for three hours. Just last week, I grabbed an 18-year-old waitress, took her to the park, and we've been making love for six straight days."

"My goodness," gasped the doctor. "Picking up all these strange girls, I hope you're using some precaution!"

"Oh, sure," chuckled the old codger. "I give them a phoney name and address."

*　　*　　*

Wanda, a recently married mountain lady, went into a fabric store and asked for some flannel to make a nightgown. She found what she wanted and requested twenty yards.

"Goodness," said the clerk, "you must be goin' to make a lot of gowns."

"No, just one," said Wanda.

"You don't need twenty yards to make one gown," insisted the clerk.

"Yes, I do," said the bride. "I'm married to an old man and he gets more fun hunting for it than he does finding it!"

*　　*　　*

Campus Coitus

What's the difference between a Clemson co-ed and a bowling ball?

You can only get three fingers in a bowling ball.

*   *   *

Why are Indiana University co-eds like turtles?

They're slow, wrinkled, and they can't get off their backs.

*   *   *

A bunch of the boys were yakking it up in the fraternity house living room, when an angry voice from the floor above cut into the din.

"Hey, you creeps, can that foul language!" yelled the angered brother. "I'm screwing a nice girl up here!"

* * *

An insatiable coed named Joan
Has a supersized dildo of bone;
   Which is why, after class,
   Though a sociable lass,
She's been known to get off on her own.

* * *

At the University of Tennessee, in an English lit course on D.H. Lawrence, the professor requested Dovie Jewell to explain the difference between fornication and adultery.

"Well," she stammered, "I've tried them both, and they seem about the same."

* * *

Did you hear about the Kansas State frosh who decided not to sign up for a course in sex education when she heard the final exam would be oral?

*   *   *

A pretty but overweight Cornell soph visited the kindly campus psychiatrist despondently to report that she thought she was losing her boyfriend.

"Why don't you diet?" asked the shrink.

"That's a neat idea," said the co-ed. "What color do you think he'd like?"

*   *   *

The physics professor turned from the blackboard and said to his class, "I defy you to name anything faster than the speed of light."

"Just one thing," said the student. "A man on his way home to his wife after seeing a stag movie."

*   *   *

Wilkens, the young physician, was bewildered by the procession of unhappy co-eds regularly visiting his office for pregnancy tests. "There seems to be something in the air this time of year that causes young girls to get pregnant," he commented to an older colleague. "What is it, I wonder?"

"Their legs," replied his friend.

*   *   *

Jef Blum, San Francisco's bombastic business consultant, gets beams out of this bauble:

A little baby stork was very upset because his mother was gone all night. He asked his father about it. "Your mother has been making people very happy," the father stork replied.

The next night the father stork was gone and the baby stork asked his mother where he was. "Your father is out making people very happy."

The next night the baby stork was gone till wee hours. When he came in the mother stork and father stork asked where he had been.

"Scaring the hell out of college kids," he replied.

There was a young co-ed named Reed
Who had an emotional need.
   So to shock her best friends,
   She went to great ends:
She stood on her head when she peed.

*   *   *

According to a recent poll of college students, the three biggest lies on campus are:
1. "God is dead."
2. "I was only holding the reefer for a friend."
3. "I'm glad you made me wait until after the wedding."

*   *   *

Did you hear about the co-ed who passed biology by giving her body to science?

*   *   *

What's the difference between a Mississippi State co-ed and a catfish?
One of them has gills and whiskers—however, the fish lives underwater.

*   *   *

An attractive sophomore at a staid Southern girls' school entered the Dean of Women's office and began to weep bitterly. "A strange man jumped me, knocked me out and violated me while I was unconscious," she sobbed. "It was terrible!"

"That is terrible," said the dean. "You missed the best part."

*   *   *

COLLEGE

*A fountain of knowledge
where all go to drink.*

*   *   *

The economics professor at an all-male university voiced his opposition to giving objective-type exams, by writing these words on the blackboard: *man, woman, sex, egg,* and *rug.* Then he asked the class to choose the word not related to the others in the group.

Most of the responses from the students were the same, but they were all surprised when he circled the word *sex.*

With a sly smile, he explained. "You can beat a rug and you can beat an egg; and you can also beat a man and a woman. But, gentlemen, you can't beat sex!"

Leered the dean to the co-ed, "My dear,
I'm intrigued by your boobs and your rear!
  When I've got you in bed,
  I'll expect you to spread—
We've an open-admissions rule here."

*　　*　　*

Did you hear about the practical Purdue co-ed who brought a negligee with fur around the hemline to keep her neck warm?

*　　*　　*

At a Bryn Mawr sorority slumber party, the sisters got to talking about the girls they knew who *put out*. Barbara, not so bright, asked, "Cheryl, what does *put out* mean?"

Cheryl replied, "Well, a girl who *puts out* is one who offers the boys something to *put it in*. . . ."

*　　*　　*

Why does Louisiana State have artificial turf on the football field instead of regular grass?

To keep the cheerleaders from grazing.

*　　*　　*

"Well," said the mother, "I see you were out with one of those wild Georgia Tech fraternity boys last night. I hope you kept your eyes open."

"I sure did," laughingly replied the girl. "Don't men look funny when they screw?"

*   *   *

A biology professor said to his class, "Can you name a part of the human body whose function is a delayed one?"

"Yes," sighed Sabrina, "the diaphragm. Mine allows me to breathe more easily the following morning."

*   *   *

Why don't Florida State co-eds drink Kool Aid?

They can't get two quarts of water in that little packet.

*   *   *

Prof: I know that girl. I had her in my class once.

Student: Couldn't you find a place with a little more privacy?

*   *   *

It was Professor Boone's wedding night. He got into bed with his bride, kissed her on the forehead, and sat up reading a book.

She fell asleep in disgust, but woke up when she felt his finger in her vagina.

"Do you want me, darling?" she cooed.

"It's all right," he replied, without looking up. "I'm only wetting my finger to turn this page.

Why do cheerleaders wear short skirts?
To make the boys "root" harder.

* * *

Did you hear about the young professor who kept eyeing and trying the lush co-eds until he ended up with a couple of dilated pupils?

* * *

There's a co-ed at State named Doreen
Who's renowned on the oral-sex scene.
  Since vibrato, it's said,
  Is the crown on her head,
She's been voted the Humcoming Queen.

* * *

What's the difference between a Colorado co-ed and a buffalo?
About 25 pounds.
How can you even it up?
Force-feed the buffalo, or shave the co-ed.

* * *

What do Memphis State co-eds put behind their ears to get a guy?
Their ankles.

* * *

Professor Lindsay was the most broad-minded instructor on campus. One morning he asked, "Venereal disease has plagued mankind for centuries. Can anyone tell me when this problem originated?"

"Like all other human troubles," a cute co-ed replied, absent-mindedly thinking back to her mythology course, "it probably sprang from Pandora's Box."

*　*　*

What's the difference between garbage and a girl from Michigan State?

At least garbage gets picked up once a week.

*　*　*

UNDERGRADUATE DRINKING SONG

It's a hell of a situation up at Yale.
It's a hell of a situation up at Yale.
　It's a hell of a situation,
　They are sunk in masturbation
For there ain't no fornication up at Yale.

Oh, the freshmen get no tail, up at Yale.
Oh, the freshmen get no tail, up at Yale.
　Oh, the freshmen get no tail,
　So they bang it on the rail.
It's the asshole of creation up at Yale.

Did you hear about the University of Miami co-ed who went to the big homecoming game and came back home with a bad case of athlete's fetus?

*   *   *

"Step into the bakery," said the pastry chef to his pretty, new U.C.L.A. assistant. "I'd like to show you my special use of shortening."

"Shortening, hell!" snapped the young co-ed. "All you want to show me is your lengthening!"

*   *   *

What's the difference between an Arkansas co-ed and a squad car?

It takes *two* squad cars to block a road.

*   *   *

On campuses all across America, venereal disease warnings are being taken very seriously by the students. Recently, the star fullback at a Midwest university wouldn't let his date go down on him, because she had an infectious smile.

*   *   *

Hadley staggered into the dorm from a heavy date, crawled into bed, pulled up the covers, and began to sink into a deep sleep. Suddenly, his roommate Lucas sat up and hollered, "You'd never guess what happened here tonight!"

"Go to hell," mumbled Hadley.

"I woke up a while ago," began Lucas, "and sensed movement nearby. First I could hear low breathing, then I felt something warm and furry against my groin. I quickly turned on the night lamp. There was our dorm mother's cat, licking me."

Hadley groaned, "What's odd about that? Puss is always loving somebody."

Lucas agreed, "Yes, but here's the unbelievable part. I picked that kitty up, swung her around in a circle, and for the first time in my young life I threw a pussy out of my bed!"

* * *

"What are you scowling about?" said Heather to her overly developed sorority roommate.

"The only trouble with a 38-inch bust is that it makes a size 34 blouse so hard to button."

* * *

What is the difference between a circus and a sorority?

A circus is an array of cunning stunts. . . .

* * *

The following riddle is provided for incoming Harvard freshmen:

What is the difference between a Cliffie and a toilet seat?
—Toilet seats are comfortable to sit on.
—You get used to the looks of a toilet seat.
—Toilet seats are easier to communicate with.
—Toilet seats warm up when you touch them.
—Toilet seats don't have droopy boobs.

* * *

WRITTEN ON A RADCLIFFE LADIES ROOM WALL

All boys who go to Harvard are fags.
(written underneath)
Except one and he's a Lesbian.

* * *

*   *   *

A student at Harvard named Brand
Thought caressing his penis was grand.
    But he viewed with distaste
    The gelatinous paste
That it left in the palm of his hand.

*   *   *

The longest, continual collegiate war between the sexes has been fought by undergraduates from Harvard and Radcliffe. The Harvard man refers to a Radcliffe woman as a "Cliffe Bitch" or a "Rad-clit."

And

"Ninety-five percent of all co-eds are beautiful. The other five percent go to Radcliffe."

"Sex at Radcliffe is like bridge—if you have a good hand, you don't need a partner."

*   *   *

The Northwestern cutie returned to the sorority house after her first breakfast date at a neighboring fraternity with her steady boyfriend. Asked what she had, she replied dreamily, "Him and eggs."

*   *   *

A big, broad-shouldered Ivy League fullback was lounging in the lobby of a New York hotel the night before a game. He spied an attractive blonde and made a play for her.

"How'd you like to get into the movies?" he asked.

"Oh," she answered, "are you from Hollywood?"

"No," he said, "but why don't we talk about it?"

This corny routine must have worked because she went with him to his room. "Look," he said after closing the door, "you take off your things here. I'll get undressed in the bathroom and when I come back you're gonna see 240 pounds of dynamite!"

The big guy went into the bathroom, took off all his clothes, and came back completely naked. "Well, how do you like it, baby? Two-hundred-forty pounds of dynamite!" he boasted, flexing his muscles.

The girl looked him over, picked up her clothes, and ran out of the room. The bellboy stopped her and said, "What's the matter?"

"There, in room 612!" she cried.

"What's in room 612?" he asked.

"Two-hundred-forty pounds of dynamite!" she screamed. "With a two-inch fuse!"

There was a co-ed from Detroit,
Who at screwing was very adroit.
    She could squeeze her vagina
    To a pin point and finer.
Or open it out like a quoit.

*   *   *

Harold, who was working as a waiter at Jenny Lake Lodge, told another Wyoming U. fraternity brother about a gag an undergrad girlfriend pulled off last semester.

"She disguised herself as a boy," explained Harold, "and joined TKE. The authorities never found out about it."

"Wait a minute," said the brother. "If this girl joined a fraternity, she would have had to dress with the guys and shower with them."

"Sure."

"Well, then, someone must have discovered she was a girl!"

"Probably," said Harold, "but who'd tell?"

*   *   *

Did you hear about the Princeton cheerleader who got her birth-control pills mixed up with her saccharin tablets?

Now she has the sweetest little baby in town?

*   *   *

What's the difference between an Arizona State University co-ed and a toilet?

A toilet doesn't follow you around for a week after you've used it.

*   *   *

The dean of women at a large Eastern university recently began a speech to the student body with these memorable words:

"The president of the university and I have decided to stop petting on campus."

*   *   *

What's the toughest thing a guy from Texas A&M does on his wedding day?

Slip the ring over the hoof.

*   *   *

A Kent State co-ed named Chris
Was scared she'd conceived from a kiss.
  So, as a precaution,
  She had an abortion,
But naught was forthcoming but piss.

*   *   *

Wilbur's classmate Kathy wanted him to get some rubbers before she'd let him do it. A bit nervous, he went to a drugstore.

"Can I help you, son?" asked the clerk.

"Well, er a, do you have any rub . . . film?"

"Sure, right over there."

Wilbur bought the film and left. After getting yelled at by Kathy, he returned to the drugstore. "Say, do you have any a er . . . baking pans?" he stammered.

Still unable to ask for what he needed, he walked out with a big baking sheet.

Enraged, Kathy screamed, "First you get film, now you've got a pan. If you don't get what you're supposed to this time, I'm going home."

Wilbur walked back into the store. "Did you forget something?" asked the druggist.

"Yes, I want some rubbers."

"*Now* you want rubbers? Tell me, sonny, are you going to take it, bake it, or make it?"

*   *   *

How do you get a Boston College co-ed through a door?

Grease the frame and dangle a Twinkie on the other side.

*   *   *

Misty attended a California state college but lived at home. One day under parental questioning, she admitted that she was pregnant, but added that she really couldn't say who was responsible.

"All right, young lady," screeched her father, "you go to your room and stay there until you can give us a more definite answer than that."

Later in the day, Misty bellowed into the den, "Hey, Dad, I think I have an idea now!"

"I should hope so," shouted back her father. "Who was it?"

"Well, I'm still not positive, but I've got it narrowed down. It's between the basketball team and the band."

*　　*　　*

Preppies are living proof that
fraternity boys fuck sheep.

Sportsmen Scorealotus

At a crucial point of the ball game at San Francisco's Candlestick Park, a fan leaped to his feet and hollered, "Go, team! Let's lick 'em!"

On the row below, Stanley lisped, "I'll buy that."

*   *   *

Barbara took her friend Eileen to see the New York Mets. It was Eileen's first time at a game.

"Say," asked Eileen, "why is he walking to first base?"

"Because," said Barbara, "he's got four balls."

"No wonder he can't run," returned Eileen.

*   *   *

Did you hear about the fellow who was hired to coach an all-girl softball team, but spent the season in the batter's box.

*   *   *

Chess has been prominent in the news lately and, as a result of the publicity, feminists are up in arms. Some militant femmes think the term *chessmen* should be changed to *chess persons*.

However, a leading authority on the game says, "The correct wording is *chess pieces*—the queen being the best piece."

*   *   *

A small-town Midwest baseball team had a live rooster for a mascot. They had a little uniform made for the rooster, who liked nothing so much as to go out now and then and knock up a few fowls.

*   *   *

A team playing baseball in Dallas
Called the umpire names out of malice.
    While that worthy had fits
    The team made six hits,
And a girl in the bleachers named Alice.

*   *   *

*   *   *

At the Orange Bowl a beautiful but obviously bleached Cuban blonde was sitting watching the Dolphins beat the Jets. Enthralled, she forgot to keep her knees crossed.

In the seats below, Rick and Steve were looking up her skirt. Rick asked, "How come that blonde has such dark pussy hair?"

"Pussy hair, nothing!" snorted Steve. "That's flies!"

*   *   *

It was a tense moment in the final game of the world series. The pitcher trotted in to home plate and spoke intently to the catcher. While thousands of spectators held their breaths, a supersensitive microphone picked up the pitcher's hurried remark, "For Christ's sake, zip up your fly! I'm getting your signals all mixed up!"

*   *   *

The luckiest athlete in sports is a baseball catcher. He can scratch his gizmo in front of 50,000 fans and not cause any raised eyebrows. He simply pretends to be passing a sign to the pitcher.

*   *   *

On his wedding night the famous athlete from a Midwest college checked into the penthouse honeymoon suite of a highrise Vegas hotel.

The bride was very shy when they were about to undress, and asked him to wait in the bathroom until she got into her nightgown. In a few minutes he called out, "Ready, dear?"

"Just a minute, honey," she replied.

Time dragged on endlessly as the college track star panted. Finally, he heard her call out "Ready, darling."

The bathroom door flew open, out flashed the athlete into the darkened bedroom, tripped over a chair, and pole vaulted out the window.

My grandfather's cock
Was too big for his jock,
So it hung ninety years by his side.
  It was long, it was fat,
  Like a big baseball bat.
It was grandfather's treasure and pride.

*   *   *

  A woman took her son to a sporting-goods store to buy him a baseball glove. She said to the clerk, "I'd like to get my son a glove."

  "That'll be $65," said the clerk.

  "Oh, I didn't want to spend that much. He's just a little boy. Is there anything else?"

  "I can give you a bat for five dollars."

  "Oh, that's fine."

  The clerk wrapped it up and said, "How about a ball for the bat?"

  "No, but I'll blow you for the glove."

*   *   *

BASEBALL BALLAD

She was only a pitcher's daughter,
but she'd let you pour it to her.

*   *   *

Why is Billie Jean King such a good tennis player?

She swings both ways.

*   *   *

"What a weekend!" the exhausted house guest exclaimed. "Mixed doubles without a letup, and then someone had to go and suggest tennis!"

*   *   *

The big senior center approached the college's star quarterback. "Hey, Cole, wanna come with us over to Penny's place? She's gonna take on everybody who shows up."

"No, thanks. A gang bang is like a buffet supper," said the scholarly backfield ace. "You stand in line to take all you want of whatever's left . . . and you usually find that the guests before you spilled sauce all over."

*   *   *

Did you hear about the basketball player who was so tall his girlfriend had to go up on him?

*   *   *

Every year a hunting club went up into the Montana hills. The members drew straws to decide who would handle the cooking, and also agreed that anyone complaining about the food would automatically replace the unlucky cook.

Realizing that after a few days no one was likely to risk speaking up, Sanderson decided on a desperate plan. He found some moose droppings and added two handfuls to the stew that night. There were grimaces around the campfire after the first few mouthfuls, but nobody said anything. Then one member suddenly broke the silence.

"Hey," he exclaimed, "this stuff tastes like moose shit . . . but good!"

A young writer was interviewing the pro-football star for his magazine. "Dan, what was your most embarrassing experience?" asked the reporter.

"When my mother caught me playing with myself," replied the gridiron hero.

"Heck, we all did that when we were kids."

"I know, but this happened yesterday!"

*　　*　　*

FOOTBALL GROUPIE

A jock absorber.

*　　*　　*

The captain of the football team walked into the athletic office to see the coach.

"Would you like to tell me your problem?" asked the pretty student receptionist. "I'll need the information for your school record."

"It's rather embarrassing," the athlete stammered. "You see, I have a very large and almost constant erection."

"Well, the coach is very busy today," she cooed, "but maybe I can squeeze you in."

*　　*　　*

The pro quarterback was petitioning the court to have his recent marriage annulled. "On what grounds?" asked the judge.

"Non-virginity!" replied the football player. "When I married her, I thought I was getting a tight end, but instead I got a wide receiver!"

*   *   *

They had a great football team at Southern High Institute of Technology—but none of the members would wear the letter sweaters.

*   *   *

She didn't know a thing about archery, but she could make her boyfriend quiver.

*   *   *

The coach was counseling his star halfback. "Derrick, you are ruining your form by trying to screw every pretty girl on campus. Now, it's my advice that when you get excited, take a cold shower."

"I've tried that," answered the team Romeo. "It not only doesn't work, but it turns off the chicks when I am balling them with my teeth chattering!"

*   *   *

OVERHEARD AT A GAY BAR

Cedric: If my fanny was a football, would
            you kick it?
Esmond: I sure would!
Cedric: Here's the stem—blow it up!

*   *   *

Who is the most worried man in the world?

It's got to be the center on the football team at the University of Greece.

*   *   *

PASSING FANCY

A queer quarterback.

*   *   *

"When Arnold gets back from one of his long trips," confided his wife, "it's like a T.V. football coverage in reverse."

"What do you mean?" asked her girl-friend.

"Instant foreplay."

*   *   *

One morning, a big she-bear raided Joe's cabin, scattered everything, tore up everything, ate everything, and ambled away.

Joe trailed her, shot her, and then noticing how much she resembled a woman, he satisfied his passion with her carcass.

Just then he noticed another hunter cowering in the branches of a nearby tree. Realizing his deed had been observed, Joe pointed his gun at the man, made him climb down, and said, "Have you ever screwed a bear?"

"No," said the hunter, "but I'm getting ready to try."

*　　*　　*

PIGSKIN PROSTIE'S PASSION

If I were the marrying kind,
And not a pay-for player,
The kind of man I'd wed
Would be a football player.
He'd touch down and I'd touch down,
We'd both touch down often.
We'd be all right
In the middle of the night
If his goal post didn't soften.

*　　*　　*

Bronkowski's wife was making a spectacle of herself at a Buffalo Bills game. She was drunk, screaming obscenities at the players on the field, and ended up sitting on a strange guy's lap inside his raccoon coat . . . bouncing up and down.

"Hey," said Bronkowski's friend, "can't you see that guy is screwing your wife?"

"Don't pay any attention," said Bronkowski. "She's drunk."

"Why the hell don't you leave her home to get drunk?"

"Yeah?" said the Polack, "then everybody'd screw her."

Bolenkowicz was a huge tackle on a small semi-pro Polish coal-miner's team in Pennsylvania. His wife was built exactly like him.

One night the two were drinking beer in a saloon, and Bolenkowicz broke his arm in a fight. His team was playing the next day so he said to his wife, "You put on uniform and sit on bench. We need the money. They no even call you to play."

She agreed.

Next day Mrs. Bolenkowicz sat on the bench in her husband's uniform. Slowly but surely all the substitutes were called upon and finally the coach sent in Mrs. Bolenkowicz.

The woman ran on the field and in the very first play she got creamed, knocked out cold. She woke up in the dressing room on the training table. Kublik, the trainer, was massaging and pounding her breasts down frantically. "Hey, what are you doing?" she groaned.

"Don't worry," said the Polack. "If I can get your balls back in place maybe I can get that pecker of yours to pop back out!"

*   *   *

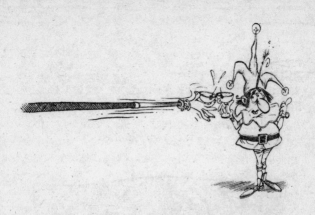

As the college football star was dressing to slip out of the girl's dormitory quickly and quietly, his sexy date said, "Don't forget to leave a contribution!"

"What do you mean by 'contribution'?" he questioned and gulped. "What the devil are you—a whore masquerading as a college girl?"

"No, darling," she snarled. "Just a business major!"

* * *

FULLBACK'S PHILOSOPHY

In the game of love we claim
There's only one reward—
It isn't how you played the game
But how often you have scored.

Servicemen
Screwevenmorethanus

Members of the American Legion were gathered in Atlantic City for their big convention. Sitting on a boardwalk bench were Master Sergeant Derman and his Korean War buddy Sergeant Stead.

"Hey," asked Derman, "do you remember the saltpeter they gave us during the war to quiet our nerves?"

"Yeah," said Stead, "what about it?"

"Well," said the Master Sergeant, "it's just beginning to work!"

* * *

First Sergeant Collins discovered Private Jennings in the barracks with a girl.

"Uh uh," stammered Jennings. "This is my sister, sarge."

"That's okay," winked the sergeant. "She used to be mine."

* * *

143

Private McBee came home on furlough, and that night he drove his girl out to lovers' lane. About 20 miles from town, they ran out of gas, so he suggested they get out and push.

She agreed. So they got out and pushed —he pushed and she pushed, he pushed and she pushed—and while they were both pushing, someone stole the car!

*　　*　　*

Lt. Col. Bellows was taken into custody by the M.P.'s. The colonel, completely naked, had been chasing a woman through the lobby of a large hotel. However, his lawyer soon had him freed on a technicality.

The army manual specifically states that an officer need not be in uniform, provided he is properly attired for the sport in which he is engaged.

*　　*　　*

A soldier on guard at Camp Shanks
Walked his post by the old water tanks.
　As he walked on the grass
　He trod hard on an ass
And heard a young lass murmur, "Thanks."

*　　*　　*

Webb, a tall, handsome major, entered the office of the commanding general and snapped to attention. He then informed the crusty old soldier, "Sir, I have secret information that one of your aides is a faggot."

"Which one?" thundered the old soldier.

"I'll tell you, sir," replied the major, "but first you'll have to kiss me."

* * *

THE MILITARY

The unqualified leading the incompetent to do the unnecessary.

* * *

P.F.C. Castillo in the South Pacific asked his C.O. for permission to go home and see his wife. The officer turned him down, and said, "With all the WAACs and WAVEs and nurses we have out here, you should be able to get yourself a little nookie."

"Sir," replied the G.I., "for two and a half years I've waved it and whacked it and nursed it; now I want to go home and have an honorable discharge."

* * *

Lt. Col. Hartnett, the air hero, arrived at Randolph A.F.B. and met the press to tell how he felt being back in the States.

"What's the first thing you're going to do, Colonel?" asked a reporter.

"Get screwed!" Hartnett replied.

The Air Force P.R. Officer calmly stepped in, "Lt. Col. Hartnett means that he's rushing back to his hometown to say a prayer for his departed comrades in the First Presbyterian Church, and to taste his mother's home-baked apple pie!"

*　　*　　*

Petty Officers Tewley and Miggins were walking down the street in Key West when a girl stuck her head out of a doorway and shouted, "Come in fellows and I'll give you something you've never had before."

"Run like hell!" said Tewley to shipmate. "She's got leprosy."

*　　*　　*

OFFICER'S MOUNT

What the GIs call a snooty girl around the army base, who reserves her favors for lieutenants or better.

*　　*　　*

Pvt. Cosgrove went to the chaplain and said, "I'm writing a letter home, and I'm stuck on something. Sir, is there a hyphen in 'hard on'?"

"Son," gasped the clergyman, "whatever are you telling your folks in that letter?"

"Just this, sir," answered the G.I. "I'm telling Mom and Dad we're finally able to attend services in your field chapel—the one we all worked so hard on."

*   *   *

Col. Siegel was about to be led before the firing squad.

"You can have five minutes of grace before you die," said the officer in charge.

"Okay," said the soldier, "bring her in."

*   *   *

Zelma, a Kentucky farm girl, was visiting her cousin LaVerna in Alabama.

"The strangest thing happened to me last week," she told her relative. "I was alone in the house and a soldier from the camp came in. Without a word he took off his cap and his coat and his pants and threw me on the bed. . . .

"Then he got up, put on all his clothes, and went out without sayin' a word. Lord only knows what that boy wanted!"

Sgts. Kent, Walker and Braden, on duty in Germany, were walking down a country road and came to a young heifer grazing in a pasture.

"Gee," said Kent. "If that was only Bo Derek."

"Damn," said Walker. "If it was only Racquel Welch."

"Hell," said Braden. "If it was only dark!"

A bunch of new women marines were sent to a predominately male base to train as keypunch operators. Several days later, an officer stopped in and asked, "How are the new hunt-'n'-peckers doing?"

Their supervisor answered, "They're not just hunt-'n'-peckers, they're finding them!"

*   *   *

Being in the service is like a good blow job.

The closer you get to discharge, the better you feel.

*   *   *

Larvel, a hillbilly in the army in Germany, was writing his girlfriend back in Tennessee a letter. He turned to Col. Mattis and said, "How do you spell *poontang*?" So the Colonel told him.

Then in a minute he turned again to his buddy and said, "How do you spell *rat*?"

Mattis told him and also asked, "What are you writing her, anyway?"

Larvel said, "I am telling her how much I want some of her poontang rat now!"

*   *   *

Sergeant Porterfield, the Marine drill instructor, rushed into the boot-camp barracks at 4:00 A.M. one freezing morning and shouted to the boots, "Everybody outside for inspection. Without your clothes on, naked."

The platoon lined up in four rows. The men gritted their teeth in the early dawn frost. Porterfield strolled down the first waving his riding crop.

Suddenly, the sergeant whacked a young recruit across the chest and shouted, "Did that hurt?"

"No, *suh*!"

"Why not?" asked the drill instructor.

"Because I'm a United States Marine, *suh*!"

The D.I. strutted down the second row and whacked another naked Marine across the buttocks. "Did that hurt?"

"No, *suh*!" answered the boot.

"Why not?"

"Because I'm a U.S. Marine, *suh*!"

Walking down the next row, the sergeant noticed a recruit with an enormous erection. The D.I. had to walk around it. Suddenly, he whacked it with the riding crop. "Did that hurt?" screamed Porterfield.

"No, *suh*!" said the boot.

"Why not?" asked the D.I.

"Because it belongs to the guy in back of me!"

TITTIE HAMMOCK

A WAVE's brassiere.

* * *

Meat-rationing did not terrify Miss Davey.
She got married to a sailor in the navy.
  For she knew between his legs
  He had ham and he had eggs,
A big weenie, and oodles of white gravy.

* * *

A navy doctor shouted at a new medic, "No! No! This is the day for blood samples. You're making fools of us in front of all these men."

"But I was doing what you told me to do."

"No, you weren't, imbecile. I said prick their fingers!"

* * *

Did you hear about the San Diego waitress who had kissed so many sailors her lips moved in and out with the tide?

* * *

During World War II, a seaman, Odell, and his English girl were strolling down lovers' lane. As they walked hand in hand, Odell pulled an orange out of his pocket and offered it to her.

"Darling, I really can't accept it," protested the girl. "Oranges are so scarce in England right now that they're reserved for small children and pregnant women."

"That's okay, honey," said the sailor. "You can take it now and then eat it on the way back."

*   *   *

"What was the rank of that navy man you were dancing with all evening at the country club?" demanded an anxious Orlando mother.

"I'm not sure," answered the daughter, "but judging by his actions, I'd say he was Chief Petting Officer."

*   *   *

S.O.S.

An old naval term that means:
Stoop Over Sport.

*   *   *

Dave Viviani, the handsome Sonoma Jack big cheese, gets giggles out of this dilly:

After inspecting the Women's Army Corps troops the major said, "Sergeant, this is disgraceful. Just look at those uniforms, why there are not two hemlines the same length. Now get over to the tailor shop and find out the reason."

"Sir, the new tailor is a man and he's been measuring from the crotch down. Some of the women go *oops*, and the rest go *aahhh*."

Jenkins and Baird were assigned to a destroyer. The second day out they struck up a conversation at mess.

"You know," said Jenkins, "the best tail I've ever had was right here on this ship."

"No shit?" said Baird.

"Well, not enough to really matter!"

*　　*　　*

There was a young sailor from Brighton
Who remarked to his girl, "It's a tight one."
　　She replied, "Shut your face,
　　You're up the wrong place;
There's plenty of room in the right one."

*　　*　　*

The guys were all gathered in the barracks and Corporal Green was telling his buddies about his night in town.

"I said to her, 'A penny for your thoughts.' And she said to me, 'A penny, hell, it's twenty-five bucks!' "

*　　*　　*

Why doesn't a sailor on leave ever pick a fat female?

He knows you can't reach the porthole with a bay window in the way.

*　　*　　*

Seaman Apprentice Garcia discovered, when he arrived home in Miami on leave, that his wife was expecting a baby at any moment. Immediately he dispatched a telegram to his commanding officer requesting an extension and explaining his reason.

His reply came quickly and consisted of the following message:

U.S. NAVY RECOGNIZES NECESSITY OF YOUR PRESENCE AT LAYING OF KEEL. CONSIDERS YOUR PRESENCE AT LAUNCHING SUPERFLUOUS.

*   *   *

Seaman Recruit Rojek was told that the ship he was on was not a real ship but a dummy in dry dock, with 40 wheels under it on each side. He was asked to put his head through the porthole to see.

"What are you talking about?" he asked, with his head out the porthole. "I don't see any *wheeeeeels*!!!"

*   *   *

THUNDERBIRD

*A parrot that eats nothing
But navy beans.*

*   *   *

Seaman Stadnicki had been marooned on a desert island for eleven years. One morning he saw a small speck on the horizon, and soon the speck turned into a beautiful blonde floating toward the beach on a barrel.

"How long have you been here?" called the girl.

"Eleven years," said the sailor.

"Oh, then I'll give you something you haven't had in a long time," said the blonde as she landed.

"Don't tell me," said the Polack, "you got beer in that barrel?"

*　*　*

During the rush hour, a sailor saw a pretty girl about to cross a street in Norfolk. Seizing the chance to be helpful as well as gallant, he ran up to her side and asked, "May I convey you to safety?"

"Definitely not," she replied, "the last time one of you swabbies convoyed me, I got torpedoed twice!"

*　*　*

Seaman Apprentice Flinn was back home after a long tour of duty and his church congregation gave him a huge homecoming dinner. In the midst of the festivities, he asked one of the ladies, "Would you pass the fugging butter?" Then, realizing what he'd said, he fled from the table and hid in the men's room.

A few minutes later, the pastor came in, put a hand on his shoulder, and said, "It's all right, son. We understand," and led him gently back to the table.

As Flinn slid back into his seat, he said politely, "Gosh, I'm sorry folks. I sure hope I don't fug up again."

*　*　*

* * *

Did you hear about the sailor who hated to get married and leave his buddies behind?

* * *

A sailor was sitting on the toilet in the head wiping himself, and examining the paper, which was all bloody.

"What's the matter," asked his buddy. "You got piles?"

"No, I was in the shower with this big black guy and I asked him what his name was. He said 'Ben Drover,' and I guess I misunderstood!"

* * *

MARINE SEX

This takes two marines and one woman. One marine and the woman engage themselves while the other marine calls the cadence.

* * *

Sgts. Micheli and Leonard, two platoon leaders, were on the phone to each other in the jungles of Vietnam.

"We got twenty cases of dysentery," said Leonard. "I don't know what to do."

"Send them over," said Micheli. "My boys'll drink anything."

Religiosis Rectalotofus

Mitchell asked his pastor if there was any sure way to quit smoking.

"Punish yourself," said the preacher. "Every time you catch yourself at it, hand the person next to you a five-dollar bill."

Mitchell started to leave, but just as he got to the front door he reached for his lighter, realized what he was doing, and handed the parson's wife a five-dollar bill.

She whispered, "Meet me in the choir loft after supper."

*   *   *

*   *   *

"When I see a monk's ass, I just
    grab it,"
Said a lazily amorous abbot.
    "Though it's vastly more fun
    To make love to a nun,
It's so hard to get into the habit."

*   *   *

Kirsten, Noreen and Sylvia passed on
and came before St. Peter. The question put
to each was, "How many times have you
cheated on your husband?"

Kirsten answered, "Once."

She was told to go walk around Paradise one time.

Noreen admitted to a couple of indis-
cretions, and her instructions were to walk
around Paradise twice.

Sylvia said, "Before answerin' the question, could I go back to earth for my jog-
ging shoes?"

*   *   *

In the Garden of Eden, 'tis said, Eve
blew her top every time Adam turned over
a new leaf.

*   *   *

Robertson opened one of the Gideon Bibles in a Los Angeles hotel room.

On the front page he read this inscription:

"If sick, read Psalm 18. If troubled about your family, read Psalm 45. If you are lonely, read Psalm 92."

He was lonely, so he opened to Psalm 92 and read it. When through, he noticed on the bottom of the page the handwritten words:

"If you are still lonely, call Hollywood 5-0394, and ask for Shanda."

* * *

In the Garden of Eden they did it in reverse. . . .

Leaf 'em and Love 'em.

* * *

Carlson was walking down a Harrisburg street with a Bible under his arm, when he met his pal Roache. "Where you headed?" asked Roache.

"Well," replied Carlson, "I've been hearing so much about Atlantic City, . . . pretty girls, strip shows, horse races and so on . . . I'm going down there and try it out."

"But what's the idea of the Bible?" asked Roache.

"If it's as good as they say it is," said Carlson, "I might stay over Sunday."

Sisters Margaret and Agatha ran out of gas on the highway and flagged down a truck to help them. "I can give you some gas, sisters," said the truck driver, "but I don't have anything to put it in."

"That's all right," said Sister Margaret. "We do. Sister and I are returning from a nursing assignment and there's a bedpan in our car."

The driver siphoned out some gasoline and went on his way.

The nuns began pouring the gas slowly and carefully from the bedpan into the tank of their car to avoid spilling any of the precious liquid.

A man driving by slowed down his vehicle to see what the women were doing and then exclaimed, "Wow, that's what I call faith!"

There was an old maid in a pew
Who said as the curate withdrew,
"I prefer the dear vicar,
He's longer and thicker.
Besides, he comes quicker than you."

*　　*　　*

Dorothy had no children. She sat on a bus, petting and cooing over her little lap dog. A priest sitting behind her leaned forward and said, "It would be better if you'd adopt a poor little orphan instead of making such a fuss over a dog."

The woman retorted, "If you'd wear your pants like you wear your collar, there wouldn't be so many poor little orphans."

*　　*　　*

Winslow, a young minister, met Jennifer in church and wooed her for several years. His conduct toward her was of the highest order.

Finally they were married, on their honeymoon, and getting ready for bed. When she came out of the bathroom, he went in. When Winslow came back, Jennifer was lying naked on the bed with her legs spread apart.

"My goodness," he exclaimed, "I didn't expect to find you in that position."

"How did you expect to find me?" asked Jennifer.

"I thought you'd be on your knees by the side of the bed," admonished the minister.

"My God, honey, let's not do it that way," she exclaimed. "That position always gives me gas on my stomach!"

* * *

Melvina Washington was sitting in the African Tabernacle church directly below Parson Powell. He looked down and gulped. The cut of her dress was such that it revealed two magnificently rounded breasts.

"Miss Washington," he whispered, "will y'all see me in mah study right after the sermon?"

When the sermon ended, Parson Powell found Melvina waiting for him. "Miss Washington," he stated, "ah just wanted to call attention to your dress and how you is exposin' yoself."

"But pahson," she interrupted, "mah boy fren says that ah is like a radio an that when he puts one in his mouth and the other in his ear, he hears heavenly music."

"Miss Washington," he said, "would you be so kind as to recline on the couch? Ah'd like to try that."

Melvina lay down and the parson put one breast in his mouth and covered the other with his ear. After a few moments he declared, "Miss Washington, Ah swear, Ah don't heah nothin'."

"But pahson," she cried, "you is not plugged in!"

*   *   *

When Adam met Eve, she said, "Put it there, Big Boy!"

*   *   *

An old-time evangelist was giving a hell-fire-and-brimstone sermon when he noticed a number of drunks and smokers in the congregation. He thundered, "Listen to me, all you cigarette suckers, you pipe suckers, you bottle suckers!"

Selwyn lifted a limp wrist and with a high voice whimpered, "Don't forget *usss*!"

*   *   *

There once was a clergyman's daughter
Who detested all boyfriends who sought her,
    Till she found one whose dong
    Was as hard and as long
As the prayers that her father had taught her.

*   *   *

*   *   *

In the hills of West Virginia the preacher was about to begin his sermon.

"Before I start, will all the women in the congregation please cross their legs!"

There was a shuffling of feet and then silence. "All right, folks, now that the gates of hell are closed, I can begin my sermon."

*   *   *

Father Riley was driving through the back woods of Tennessee when he got a flat tire. He didn't have a jack in the trunk of the car and so the poor man was stuck in the boondocks.

Suddenly, from behind a clump of trees stepped a burly man well over six-feet tall. He saw the priest's plight and opened the trunk of the car for the spare. He then picked up the rear of the car with one hand and changed the tire with the other.

Upon tightening the last lug he said, "Well, there you are, Father!"

"Are the lugs on tight enough?"

"You bet," answered the man. "Tight as a nun!"

"Well, then you better give them another turn!"

*   *   *

Dugan and Rooney died and went to heaven. St. Peter greeted them and asked Dugan, "Did you ever commit adultery?"

"Never!" shouted the Irishman.

Dugan was given a Cadillac to ride in.

St. Peter then asked Rooney who replied, "Only once in a rare, rare while."

He was presented with a new Chevrolet.

A short while thereafter, Dugan started laughing. "What's so funny?" asked Rooney.

"Look over there," blurted Dugan. "There's our priest on roller skates!"

Adam was the first bookkeeper. . . .
He turned the leaf to make an entry.

*　　*　　*

A Born-Again Christian named Claire
Was having her first love affair.
　As she climbed into bed
　She reverently said,
"I wish to be opened with prayer."

*　　*　　*

Sisters Elizabeth, Josephine and Frances were tidying up Father Gannon's quarters.

"I think Father Gannon has some bad habits," said Sister Elizabeth. "The last time I was here I found a bottle of whiskey and so I took it and peed in it."

"Oh, that isn't all," said Sister Josephine. "The last time I was here, I found some rubber things in his drawer. I took a pin and poked holes in them!"

Sister Frances fainted.

*　　*　　*

SEXTON'S PSALM

She was only a chaplain's daughter, but you couldn't put anything pastor.

*　　*　　*

*   *   *

When Adam saw that he and Eve
were different, he split the difference.

*   *   *

On the Cleveland outskirts, a wife-
swapping party was going on full swing.
Reverend Rawlins, the crusading minister,
planned to put an end to this kind of thing,
and showed up at the house. He rang the
doorbell and, when the man of the house
opened the door, the minister said, "Er, I
was told you had a, er, party here tonight."

"We do," said the man. "We're playing
guessing games right now. The women are
blindfolded, trying to guess the men's names
by feeling their pricks. You ought to come
on in, Reverend, your name's been guessed
eight times already."

*   *   *

Moses returned from the mountain and
gathered his people to give them the message from God.

"I've got good news and bad news.
The good news is—I got him down to ten!
The bad news is—adultery is still in there."

*   *   *

A pastor predicting man's doom
Was exceedingly fond of the womb.
  He thought nothing finer
  Than the human vagina,
So he kept three or four in his room.

*　　*　　*

How did they prove Jesus was Jewish?

—He lived with his mother till he was 32.
—He went into his father's business.
—His mother thought he was God.
—And he thought his mother was a virgin.

*　　*　　*

Did you hear about the old rabbi who's performed so many circumcisions that he's popularly known as Max the Knife?

*　　*　　*

Why does the Pope take a shower with swimming trunks?
He hates to look down on the unemployed.

*　　*　　*

Ginty, Kincaid, and Nolan, three seminarians, were about to undergo their final test before ordination. An elderly priest led them into a luxurious room, told them to strip and then tie a small bell to their organs. Suddenly, a voluptuous, blonde stripper entered the room and one bell *ding-a-linged* furiously.

"To the showers, Ginty!" barked the old priest.

Then, as the girl tantalizingly undressed, the father heard *ding-a-ling, ding-a-ling*.

"Too bad, Kincaid. The showers for you, too."

Finally alone with the naked dancer, Nolan watched as the girl writhed seductively about him, yet he somehow remained calm and the bell silent.

"Praise the Lord and congratulations, Nolan!" shouted the priest. "You made it! Now, go join those weaker souls in the showers."

Ding-a-ling.

*   *   *

Did you hear they're gonna let nuns start dating?

But they have to wear Cross-Your-Heart bras and No-Nonsense pany hose.

*   *   *

Father Duffy was sent to a small Eskimo village in the coldest part of Alaska. Six months later the Bishop paid him a visit.

"How do you like it up here among the Eskimos?" he asked.

"Oh, just fine," replied the priest. "As long as I have my rosary and my vodka, I don't care how cold it is."

"I'm glad to hear it. Say, I could go for a bit of that vodka myself right now."

"Absolutely. Rosary! Would you bring us two vodkas?"

Eve wore a fig leaf. What did Adam wear?
He wore a hole in it.

*   *   *

The high-school cheerleader confessed
to the kindly old priest that she'd been having sex with her boyfriend in the front seat
of his car every night for the past two months.

"Don't you think you've been doing
something wrong?" admonished the cleric.

"I guess you're right," she mumbled.
"Maybe it would be more comfortable in
the back seat."

*   *   *

When Sister Constance came to tell the
Mother Superior that she had sinned with a
man and wished to do penance so she could
be forgiven, the Mother Superior began pack-
ing a suitcase.

"Oh, please don't put me out!" cried
the young nun. "Where will I go? What
will I do?"

"I'm not putting you out," said the
Mother Superior. "It's me that's leaving.
For thirty years here it's been nothing but
screwing and forgiving, screwing and forgiving. Beginning now, I'm through doing
the forgiving, and I'm going to get in on
some of the screwing before it's too late!"

Roxanne, a good-looking school teacher, was confessing to young Father Boyle. "Oh, Father," she stated, "I must confess a terrible sin. I called a man a dirty sonofabitch."

"Such an act," soothed the priest, "must have had great provocation. What did he do, my child?"

"Oh," she answered, "I can't tell you."

He put his arm around her. "Did he do this?" he asked.

"Much worse," she replied.

He cupped her breast in his hand. "Did he do this?"

"Much worse."

He then put his hand on her knee. "Did he do this?"

"Oh, much worse."

He then slid his hand upward until it came in contact with her hidden charms. "Did he do this, my child?"

Oh, Father, much worse."

Now Boyle pulled out his rod and shoved it to the hilt between her legs, asking, "Did he do this, my child?"

"Much worse."

"And how," he demanded, "could it be any worse?"

"Oh, Father!" she replied. "He gave me a dose of the clap."

"Why," shouted the priest, "the dirty sonofabitch!"

Did you hear about the nun who was two monks behind in her period?

*   *   *

A lecherous curate of Leeds
Was discovered one day in the weeds.
   Astride a young nun,
   He said, "Christ, this is fun—
Far better than telling one's beads."

*   *   *

Sisters Patricia, Theresa, Lucille and Agnes entered a liquor store and ordered a bottle of bourbon.

"Come now, sisters," said the owner, "you shouldn't be drinking hard liquor."

"It's not for us," said Sister Patricia. "This is for the Mother Superior's constipation."

He sold them the bottle and the women left. Later, as the owner closed up the store, he discovered the four nuns sitting in a car around back guzzling the booze like sailors.

"Ladies, I'm shocked," said the man. "You told me that the booze was for Mother Superior's constipation!"

"It is," said Sister Margaret. "When she hears about this, she'll shit!"

*   *   *

Other books by Larry Wilde

The Official Bedroom/Bathroom Joke Book
More the Official Smart Kids/Dumb Parents
  Joke Book
The Official Book of Sick Jokes
More the Official Jewish/Irish Joke Book
The Last Official Italian Joke Book
The Official Cat Lovers/Dog Lovers
  Joke Book
The Official Dirty Joke Book
The *Last* Official Polish Joke Book
The Official Golfers Joke Book
The Official Smart Kids/Dumb Parents
  Joke Book
The Official Religious/Not So Religious
  Joke Book
More The Official Polish/Italian Joke Book
The Official Black Folks/White Folks
  Joke Book
The Official Virgins/Sex Maniacs Joke Book
The Official Jewish/Irish Joke Book
The Official Polish/Italian Joke Book

   and in hardcover

THE COMPLETE BOOK OF ETHNIC
  HUMOR
HOW THE GREAT COMEDY WRITERS
  CREATE LAUGHTER
THE GREAT COMEDIANS TALK ABOUT
  COMEDY

ABOUT THE AUTHOR

Larry Wilde, the world's best selling humorist, was born in Jersey City, spent two years in the U.S. Marine Corps and then graduated from the University of Miami (Fla.). He began his career in show business as a standup comedian, playing the nation's nightclubs and theaters and appearing on television commercials and sitcoms.

Mr. Wilde has appeared on the bill with such stars as Ann-Margret, Debbie Reynolds, Pat Boone, Andy Williams, and many others. He's done acting roles on *Rhoda, Sanford & Son, Mary Tyler Moore* and performed on Carson, Griffin and Douglas.

Larry's two serious works on comedy technique *The Great Comedians Talk About Comedy* (Citadel) and *How The Great Comedy Writers Create Laughter* are recognized as the definitive works on the subject and are used as college textbooks.

Mr. Wilde's 33 books are now read in every English-speaking land and have been translated into four other languages. With sales of over 8 million, his "Official" joke books have become the largest selling humor series in the history of publishing.

Larry Wilde is in constant demand as a speaker on Humor by clubs, corporations and universities. When he is not traveling about the country on speaking engagements Larry and his wife Maryruth (author of four books) live on the Northern California coast.